Why We Garden

Why We Garden

The art, science, philosophy
and joy of gardening

Claire Masset

BATSFORD

First published in the United Kingdom in 2023
by B.T. Batsford Ltd
43 Great Ormond Street
London WC1N 3HZ
An imprint of B.T. Batsford Holdings Ltd

ISBN 9781849947565

A CIP catalogue record for this book is available from the British Library.

30 29 28 27 26 25 24 23
10 9 8 7 6 5 4 3 2 1

Reproduction by Rival Colour Ltd, UK
Printed and bound by Toppan Leefung Printing International Ltd, China

CONTENTS

INTRODUCTION

There are so many reasons not to garden. It's hard work. It's time-consuming. It can be tediously repetitive. Sometimes it's even a little degrading. What other pastime has you on your hands and knees for hours? What is this strange pull that draws us to the soil? Why are we so keen to get our hands dirty? Most of us don't need to garden. We do it because we enjoy it. In fact, we love it so much that – like Vita Sackville-West – we are willing to suffer and sacrifice for the sake of it.

More and more people are taking up gardening. Even those without gardens. Even those with busy, hectic lives, very little time or money. Even those suffering with physical or mental health problems. This says something about its singular appeal.

I wanted to explore the enigma that is our obsession with growing things: this deep, earthy passion that binds us as human beings; this unbroken thread that connects us to our ancestors. It turns out there is a lot more to gardening than meets the eye. It isn't just about having beautiful flowers or harvesting fruit and veg. Just like the soil on which it relies, gardening is rich and life-giving, in far more ways than the obvious.

Arranged in themed chapters, this book uncovers the many – sometimes wonderfully contradictory – reasons why people take up gardening and become hooked on it. Within its pages you'll meet a varied cast of characters: famous philosophers, artists and writers such as Epicurus, Monet and Orwell; not-so-famous guerrilla gardeners,

'I have broken my back,
my finger-nails, and
sometimes my heart,
in the practical pursuit of
my favourite occupation.'

VITA SACKVILLE-WEST

psychologists and scientists; and everyday gardeners like you and me. Each shines their own brilliant light on the topic.

George Orwell once said: 'Outside my work the thing I care most about is gardening.' His diaries show the daily attention he lavished on his plot and reveal, between the lines, something of its grounding effect. I love the fact that this advocate of plain English and documenter of gritty social realities was equally unpretentious in his personal pursuits: a man of the earth, in touch with the fundamentals of life. Gardeners know that there is more joy to be had from a patch of soil than virtually anything else.

Monet became so obsessed with his garden that he spent the last 43 years of his life painting it. He described Giverny as his 'most beautiful masterpiece'. But as we'll see, beauty was only part of its appeal. Something deeper was at work: a spiritual undertow that can affect all gardeners. Gardens are potent places, rich in symbolism and transformative atmosphere, and the near-alchemy of plant growth places them on the edge of the miraculous.

In Ancient Greece, the philosopher Epicurus named his thinkers' community near Athens, The Garden. In this verdant sanctuary, he and his followers found their personal *ataraxia*, or peace of mind. It's something we modern-day gardeners can relate to. Whatever the size of your plot, no space is too small, or indeed too challenging, to become an oasis of peace and plants – perhaps the closest thing to heaven you will experience. Consider, for instance, the artist Hester Mallin, who turned her balcony on the 23rd floor of a tower block in East London into a plant-packed paradise, filled with over 100 different specimens. It was her very own country garden, 70 metres in the sky.

I have – at times sheepishly – peppered the book with my own experiences in the hope that my little horticultural epiphanies will chime with yours. Gardening is often solitary work, and yet its simple practice connects us to a worldwide community of plant lovers. In this divisive world, it is a bond worth cherishing. As gardeners, we can be thankful for having something that answers so many of our deep human needs: the need for inspiration, beauty, nature, refreshment, exercise, solace, connection, hope, and so much more. And, just like life, gardening is filled with exciting contradictions. It is both enriching and humbling, freeing and enslaving, quieting and stimulating, consoling and heart-breaking. How could it ever be boring?

Research now proves what we have sensed for hundreds if not thousands of years: gardening helps us lead happier and healthier lives. Increasingly – through volunteer-run projects such as community gardens and mental-health charities – it is becoming a force for social and environmental change. Once a benign Sunday-afternoon pursuit, gardening is now helping to create a better world. We are becoming garden activists. We are saying no to peat, chemical weedkillers and harmful pesticides. We are swapping seeds and saving water. Some of us are planting up previously barren spaces where nature and people can thrive.

Mirabel Osler, one of the most perceptive garden writers whose words I have shamelessly quoted throughout this book, once posed the question: 'Why garden?' In jest, she replied: 'God knows.' This is my humble attempt at a slightly longer answer.

Beauty

'I must have flowers, always, and always.'

CLAUDE MONET

Monet didn't have just any flowers though; his artist's eye and horticultural knowledge told him which plants to select and where to put them to create a garden which was, quite simply, beautiful.

Isn't that what all gardeners want – a mini Giverny? Not a smaller, facsimile version, but what it represents: a satisfying creative endeavour, a visual delight. Monet, the ultimate artist-gardener, loved his garden perhaps even more than his painting. For the last 43 years of his life, it was his inspiration, his joy, his world. But it was also, he confessed, his 'most beautiful masterpiece'.

Our natural desire to create beauty is nowhere better served than in a garden, and this is despite gardening's many challenges. It is the most difficult art to get right. To be successful, you need to create a complete experience: one that you can look at, like a painting, but also walk around. A garden is a space you inhabit. It envelops you, not just with its physical boundaries, but with its spirit – a distinct nature incorporating movement, light and sound, which the gardener has helped to fashion. There are other difficulties too, from the vagaries of the weather and the threat of disease, to the fact that gardens are ever-changing and therefore never complete.

Thankfully, gardening is also the most forgiving art. Nature will always be more or less beautiful, whichever way you choose to mix its jewels. Unlike the painter, you are not creating something out of (virtually) nothing. A gardener's palette is already furnished with ready-made works of natural art.

According to the *grande dame* of gardening, Gertrude Jekyll, sometimes all it takes is 'to show some delightful colour-combination without regard to the other considerations that go to the making of a more ambitious picture' (*Colour in the Flower Garden*, 1908). Two plants happily juxtaposed can create a splendid little scene. Old-fashioned roses and catmint, tulips and forget-me-nots, climbing roses and clematis – all are classic duos, but the options are endless.

Think how effective containers can be. Your pot is your 'frame'. Here you can concentrate all your creative energy on a few plants, minimizing the risk of failure and increasing the potential for pleasing effect. It's a myth that you need a big plot to create something stunning. Your garden/patio/balcony/allotment/studio flat is never too small to be beautiful. Garden beauty is never dependent on size. In fact, it's the opposite. The larger the garden, the more room for error, the more need for upkeep and expense. 'In a small garden there is less fear of dissipated effort, more chance of making friends with its inmates, more time to spare to heighten the beauty of its effects.' Wise words from the Arts and Crafts architect and lover of cottage gardens, J. D. Sedding (*Garden-Craft Old and New*, 1891).

Gertrude Jekyll, like Monet, was an artist. Although she didn't reach Monet's level of renown with her painting (she had to give up all aspirations of becoming a fine artist due to deteriorating eyesight), Jekyll was one of the most prolific garden designers of her time, creating over 400 gardens in Europe and the United States. Many of these are sadly lost, but a few – such as Hestercombe in Somerset, Upton Grey in Hampshire and her own home Munstead Wood in Surrey – have been restored. And Jekyll was a productive writer, penning 15 books and over a thousand articles. She became a vocal exponent of 'gardening for art's sake' and believed that gardening should be seen a fine art. She compared plants to a box of paints. 'Planting ground is painting a landscape with living things,' she writes in her first book, *Wood and Garden: Notes and Thoughts, Practical and Critical, of a Working Amateur* (1899). To Jekyll, a garden should be 'a treasure of well-set jewels'.

How do you create such a treasure? 'Try and learn from everybody and from every place. There is no royal road,' she advises. Your gardening journey is likely to take you from one style to another as your taste develops. And this is no bad thing. Like everything in life, there is beauty in variety and a strange satisfaction in the quest for an elusive perfection. Every year your plot holds the promise of something different, something better, something even more beautiful.

Look at other gardens. You will sharpen your eye and find out what you like and don't like. Study plants – their leaves, flowers, textures, shapes and personalities – and you will discover a wealth of horticultural options. Delight in the aesthetic and have the audacity to experiment.

Some gardeners look for simplicity, others want complexity. While there are those who praise the untidy romance of a cottage garden, others need clean lines and neat edges. While some strive for a sophisticated blend of contrasts, other gardeners seek purity and coherence. There are as many incarnations of horticultural beauty as there are great gardens. How thrilling to think that right now, someone somewhere is developing a new style of gardening of which we are not yet aware.

Sensitive souls should rejoice, for although they feel pain more intensely, their enjoyment of all that is soul-enhancing in life is more profound. 'Like the musician, the painter, the poet, and the rest, the true lover of flowers is born, not made. And he is born to ... joy that is tranquil, innocent, uplifting and unfailing,' writes American poet and garden maker Celia Thaxter in her lyrical memoir, _An Island Garden_ (1894).

Jewels there were aplenty in her windswept plot on the isle of Appledore, off the coast of Maine. Here, in the second half of the 19th century, Thaxter planted a small cutting garden, with flowers arranged not by colour or according to any grand design, but by height and in rows and blocks. She grew mostly annuals, always from seed, and loved simple blooms such as marigolds, sunflowers, nasturtiums, pinks and poppies. The attraction of her garden, with its haphazard and vibrant colour combinations, was nothing like that of a subtly graduated Jekyll border, or indeed Monet's luminous arrangements. And yet it was full of its own charms and pleased its creator immensely (and so too Thaxter's friend, the artist Childe Hassam, who created Impressionist views of the garden, which have been compared to Monet's paintings of his own garden).

There is an added delight to cutting gardens. The pleasure they offer outside is redoubled when the gardener makes their selection and goes on to create exquisite indoor scenes, which is exactly what Celia Thaxter did. The rooms of her cottage, also evocatively painted by Childe Hassam, were filled with vases – often single stems, or just a small handful of one type of flower, in each vase.

*****

Monet, Thaxter and Jekyll sought aesthetic delight above all else in their gardens. It is one of the biggest motivators for many gardeners. Why do we seek beauty? Philosophers have pondered this question for centuries and, from the 19th century, psychologists have too. Even more recently neuroscientists have joined the fold. Since the late 1990s a new field of study known as neuroaesthetics has focused on understanding beauty from a neurological perspective. Studies led by Semir Zeki, Professor of Neuroaesthetics at University College London, suggest that our experience of different kinds of beauty – whether it be music, painting or even mathematical equations – produces the same patterns of activity in parts of the brain associated with pleasure and romantic love.

We know from experience that beauty can transfix its beholder. It stops us in our tracks and produces a wonderful feeling of elation and enchantment – almost akin to a revelation. There is something comforting and invigorating about such moments. They are both a shot in the arm and a balm for the soul.

When we encounter beauty, other considerations disappear; we attend to it with all our being. It takes us away from our humdrum thoughts, our chores and our worries. Such an experience contains the reassurance that all is right with the world and also produces a heightened sense of belonging. 'Somehow the boundary between our self and the world shifts and we feel more alive in the moment of flourishing that it offers. Although the experience may be fleeting, beauty leaves a trace in the mind that survives its passing,' writes psychiatrist and psychotherapist Sue Stuart-Smith in her outstanding study of the relationship between gardening and mental health, *The Well Gardened Mind* (2020).

And there's more. Garden beauty, unlike fine art, literature and architecture, is by its very nature impermanent. When you look at a painting or read a poem, it is there – solid, immutable, 'set in stone'. You can always come back to it. Gardens refuse to stay still. Because of their transience and aliveness, they seem to demand our immediate attention. The border that reaches its peak of perfection, the meadow filled with wild flowers, the blossoming tree: if you don't take it in now, the moment will soon be gone. Being aware that a garden's appeal is ephemeral redoubles its effect. It's a bit like being parent to a young child. You look at him, asleep in his bed, and stare in wonder, knowing that his current sweetness will inevitably change. In its fleetingness, the moment, tinged with a premonition of nostalgia, is so beautiful it moves you to tears. Beauty – in all its miracle forms – overwhelms you with emotion.

Celia Thaxter, on her windswept island garden, knew this feeling well. Her memoir captures the rapture she experiences over the course of a year, all because of her flowers. 'The very act of planting a seed in the earth has in it to me something beautiful,' she writes. Monet devoted his career to painting the ever-shifting effects of light on the natural world. Until the end of his life, he would walk around his garden two or three times a day, delighting in its subtle changes. To enhance its mutability, from the outset Monet designed Giverny so that it would provide a kaleidoscope of colours, textures and shapes through the seasons. Frothy cherry blossom, cheerful mounds of aubretia, bright tulips and poppies, romantic peonies and roses, carpets of nasturtiums and – of course – his famous water lilies: these were some of the many gems that punctuated the garden's calendar. Monet, the consummate plantsman and nature-lover, once admitted: 'I perhaps owe having become a painter to flowers.' No wonder he ended up painting nothing but his garden.

*****

If you're a beginner gardener, glossy magazines, gorgeous coffee-table books and dreamy Instagram feeds may weigh heavily on you: those picture-perfect creations where nothing is out of place. All those exquisite borders. All that lush, healthy growth. How can I possibly achieve all that?

Perfection is at best momentary and often deceptive. These photos should be seen for what they are: artistic renditions of – yes, beautiful – gardens, enhanced via the lens (and possibly filters) of a deft photographer. Outside the photograph's tightly constructed frame all may not be so perfect. The shot was probably taken at 'peak beauty' – at a time of year when everything in that garden comes together and at a time of day best suited to making the most of these assets (often at dawn, when the light is just right and most of us are asleep). So, relax, and focus your own gardening lens. You, too, can achieve pockets of beauty in your plot, while the rest of it is not quite as under control as you might want it to be.

Garden beauty takes many forms. Remembering that is freeing. This reminds me of La Louve in the South of France, a terraced garden created by the Hermès textile designer Nicole de Vésian in the late 1980s and 1990s. She had never gardened before, but she still created a masterpiece. La Louve has very few flowers – whatever blooms is incidental. Its beauty lies in the juxtaposition of topiarized shrubs and trees: a sculptured tapestry of green and silver shapes, whose contours are picked out by the Provence sun. It is a thoroughly personal garden and yet perfectly in tune with the landscape, relying on tough, drought-resistant local plants, such as lavender and rosemary, cistus and arbutus.

Inspiration is one thing, creation is another, and a lot more fun. In my experience, it takes time to let go of the idea that there is a right way to create a garden. I'm still not there yet. But every year I break more rules, play it less safe and give myself permission to make mistakes. While I naturally err towards pastel shades, I also know how much I enjoy seeing brighter blooms in other gardens. And so I push myself out of the confines of my narrow, self-imposed repertoire. Next year my dahlias won't all be pink and cream – some will be purple and orange. But, for now at least, I draw the line at pillar-box red.

The brilliantly candid garden writer Mirabel Osler writes in *A Breath from Elsewhere: Musings on Gardens* (1998): 'As for Good Taste, that overbearing tyrant that sends the inexperienced gardener into a spin – forget it. There is absolutely nothing intrinsic about good taste in gardens: it's as fickle as fashion.'

Other people's gardens can be inspiring, but don't let them paralyze or restrict you. Taste is whatever you want your garden to be. 'Go for what you want, not for what you are told you want. Whatever nourishes your impulses should be your launching pad ... Anything, anything please, to get away from bland conformity nourished on caution.' Thank you, Mirabel, for these liberating words.

*****

Although we may never design a garden 'worthy' of a magazine feature, in our pursuit of beauty we can have fun expressing ourselves. Give 100 people the same plot and you'll end up with 100 different gardens. Not only is there satisfaction in having a garden that is unique, there's also the possibility that yours could turn out to be truly special.

Whatever their style, the best plots are full of character and reveal something of their creators. Last year, one of the best gardens I visited took me by surprise. It wasn't grand or well known. It was a private 1-acre (0.4-ha) garden in deepest Dorset, opened for just one weekend through the National Garden Scheme. I went on a whim. My first impression was a sense of jarring. Something in my head told me it wasn't quite right; the word kitsch crossed my mind. Surely those orange rudbeckias didn't go with that peachy-pink rose? *How could they* mix white nicotiana with orangey-brown heleniums? What *were* they thinking? But then I saw the bigger picture, walked around a little more and realized it was utterly brilliant. The garden jolted me out of my preconceived – and yes, snobbish (thank you, garden magazines) – notion of what a 'beautiful' garden should be. Here was a proudly idiosyncratic gem. Just like your garden should be.

Novice, untrained gardeners have one advantage over the knowledgeable and the professional. A bit like outsider artists, they have few prejudices. This opens the door for real creation, unaffected by garden history, design or 'good taste'. And history has shown that amateur gardeners can create beautiful gardens.

One of the most famous of these is Margery Fish. She came to gardening in her mid-forties, when she and her husband Walter bought East Lambrook Manor in Somerset in 1937. Over the next 30 years, and with no horticultural training, she transformed her 2-acre (0.8-ha) 'wilderness of a garden' into a plant-packed paradise and unwittingly redefined the cottage-garden style. It combined a number of principles that we still hold dear today: a good bone structure of hard landscaping and evergreens; ground-cover plants to reduce weeding; a mix of shrubs, perennials and bulbs for year-round interest; lots of cottage-garden flowers; and a loose, natural approach to planting.

By the late 1950s, Fish was opening East Lambrook Manor to the public and writing books about her experience as a gardener. 'Of course we made mistakes, endless mistakes, but at least they were our own, just as the garden was our own. However imperfect the result there is a certain satisfaction in making a garden that is like no one else's,' she writes in her first book, *We Made a Garden* (1956). She went on to write another seven gardening books and hundreds of articles. Her fresh, honest approach made people feel it was okay to have a go, and that self-expression was all-important. Her relaxed gardening ethos (one of her books is called *Carefree Gardening*) suited a new generation of gardeners who could no longer rely on paid staff to keep everything trim and tidy. Today, East Lambrook Manor is still as beautiful as ever, thanks to its owners Gail and Mike Werkmeister and head gardener Mark Stainer, who has kept the spirit of Margery Fish alive for over 45 years.

*****

Horticultural self-expression involves an exercise of the imagination, which means that gardening time is also spent indoors, thinking of what *could* be. This 'picturing' is usually the precursor to actual creation, but it needn't be. The great thing about this type of gardening is that it allows all kinds of flights of fancy. It's a chance to dream, scheme and let go of real-life constraints such as time, money or plot size.

Many of us spend as much time conceiving our garden as we do actually in it. This is what we do when it's raining, snowing, freezing or just too cold or dark. The beauty generated by this 'mind-gardening' can be just as entrancing as an actual garden, if not more. Dreams of gardens can be dazzling collages of all sorts of influences that come together in the mind's eye, either layered onto your own plot or just pure, overblown fantasy. For a few minutes, hours or even weeks (especially if you put pen to paper), you can revel in this make-believe plot. Sometimes you do eventually make it real, so that your dream becomes a reality.

Michael Pollan's wonderfully meditative book, *Second Nature* (2003), is similar in spirit and theme to Margery Fish's *We Made a Garden*. In a series of essays, he describes the development of his plot and his gardening philosophy. In the introduction, he writes: 'This book is the story of my education in the garden. The garden in question is actually two, one more or less imaginary, the other insistently real.' To begin with 'much separates' these two gardens, but slowly, his real garden catches up with his dream garden.

Winter is a fruitful time for mind-gardening. Staring at seed packets in my local garden centre or leafing through catalogues, I am easily lured into visions of gorgeous cutting gardens reminiscent of flower paintings by Klimt, where every inch of canvas is covered in blooms (see especially his *Farm Garden with Sunflowers*, 1912). Selecting seeds is fun, exhilarating even. For me it's the starting point of a glorious floral picture.

When I dig over my patch in the winter, I wipe the slate clean. It's the chance for a completely new painting. I love this opportunity to create something from scratch and unique every year, using just a few seeds. I think Gertrude Jekyll would approve of my artistic intent, if not its results. My plot is far too small for all the blooms I'd like, but for half an hour or half a day, I can fantasize about growing a variety of sunflowers, zinnias, dahlias, cosmos, cornflowers, sweet peas, nigellas, poppies, scabious and strawflowers. I know I'll only be able to sow a few, but there's a thrill in being swept away in the reverie. And there's pleasure in refining my choice down to a handful of packets, safe in the knowledge that there is always next year for the others.

Mind-gardening allows you to imagine the garden of your dreams – the most beautiful, stunning plot you could ever wish for. This exercise feeds your creative muscle, but it's also good for the soul. Even if you don't own a garden or the perfect plot, you can revel in visions of beauty. As the Indian author Ruskin Bond puts it: 'Yes, I'd love to have a garden of my own – spacious, and full of everything that is fragrant and flowering. But if I don't succeed never mind – I've still got the dream.' (*Rain in the Mountains*, 1996). Whether in dreams or reality, elusive or real, garden beauty is worth striving for.

Work

'I have only done one sensible thing in my life – to cultivate the ground.'

VOLTAIRE

Voltaire, the great 18th-century French philosopher, writer and historian, admits that gardening is the best thing he has ever done. Forget all other pursuits: working the soil is what matters. His famous phrase, 'Il faut cultiver son jardin' ('We must cultivate our garden'), has been variously interpreted, but still holds true today. These are not his words but those of his character, Candide, in the novel of the same name. At the end of his impossibly adventurous travels, Candide meets an old man whose focus in life is tending his garden with his children. The man tells him: 'Our labour preserves us from three great evils: weariness, vice and want.' Reflecting on this, Candide says to his friends: 'All I know is that we must cultivate our garden.' The book ends with him and his companions settling on a small farm. Having spent so much time travelling the world trying to find love and answers to life's great questions, Candide realizes that contentment can be found on one's doorstep, from working the land.

There is a broader philosophical meaning to Candide's words. Instead of trying to seek answers, power, wealth or love, we should focus on what's close at hand, live a peaceful life and mind our own business.

Voltaire was making a point about what he considered the foolish optimism and philosophical systems of his age. But he was also saying, simply: tend your own patch. On a few square yards, you can make a difference – and this is the best use of your time.

In the last 20 years of his life, Voltaire enacted (albeit on a grand scale) his hero's message. He grew fruit and vegetables, kept bees and planted thousands of trees, many with his own hand. He once claimed: 'He who tills a field, renders a better service to mankind than all the scribblers in Europe.' Quite a statement for someone who wrote 2,000 books and pamphlets and over 20,000 letters.

Gardening is hard work. It is 'labour', as Voltaire writes. It causes backache, sore knees and rough hands. Why do we put ourselves through such hardship when we don't have to? Nowadays, not many people actually need to garden. And yet, like Candide, whose 'little farm yielded a great deal', we realize that there is joy – and much else besides – to be found in this kind of work.

When you work with the soil, you're immediately – literally – grounded. Take weeding: there you are, on your hands and knees, in contact with the earth. All gardeners love dirt; it is our medium – the glue that binds us to our plants and makes everything happen. Whether soft and friable, hard and unyielding or damp and heavy, we are drawn to it like a duck is to water.

Weeding is tedious, repetitive, sometimes backbreaking work, but it is also strangely satisfying and energizing. I always think I won't enjoy it, but after a while I'm drawn into a rhythm that keeps me going. What starts off as a chore turns into vivifying exercise. After an hour or so, I have cleared a patch of ground of its enemies – and I feel cleansed too.

Something about the physicality of gardening is reassuring and humanizing. In this crazy, overconnected yet detached digital age,

gardening brings us back to reality. Many of us do little else with our hands than tap a keyboard all day long. Practising manual skills – becoming good at them, taking pride in them – brings proper, life-affirming fulfilment. And while gardening roots us in the here and now, it also links us to our human past. We may not be conscious of it in the moment, but we are doing the same jobs, often using the same tools that our ancestors have relied on for hundreds, if not thousands, of years. Gardening reminds us that we are human.

Weeding, digging, pruning, watering, hoeing – most gardening tasks have simplicity embedded in them. They're based on straightforward cause and effect. If I do this, then this will happen. All I need is my hands (or feet) and a tool. It's all so much more straightforward than computers, spreadsheets, programs and systems. You can't easily multi-task while gardening. You can only weed out a single plant in one go, prune one branch at a time. Your attention isn't overwhelmed by messages, notifications or alerts popping up on your screen.

The moment I grab hold of my trowel's wooden handle something inside me is both calmed and set in motion. It's like a metaphoric deep breath. I have entered the calming realm of gardening. It marks the transition into a less complicated world. And despite the chores and physical labour, it feels like freedom.

It's no wonder we turn to gardening not as work but as relief. 'By the time I was an adult I had come to need regular contact with the soil. I still do,' admits gardener, writer and broadcaster Monty Don in *The Jewel Garden* (2004). 'If I go for a few days without gardening – not telly-gardening but proper everyday digging, planting or weeding – I become restless and dissatisfied.' The tyranny of our desk-based jobs can be overcome by a few hours in the garden. Of course, physical exercise can provide a similar release, but gardening has the added benefit of being creative, purposeful and productive. As our old friend Mirabel Osler writes in *A Gentle Plea for Chaos* (1989): 'There can be no other occupation like gardening in which, if you were to creep up behind someone at their work, you would find them smiling.'

*****

Isn't it strange that we can counter the daily grind with yet more work? Gardening is the antidote to our increasingly sedentary and digital lives, but it is also a brilliant boredom-buster and hugely empowering – emancipating even.

In the not-so-distant past, wealthy women weren't allowed to do proper gardening. It was considered inappropriate and unnecessary. Why on earth would they want to? Elizabeth von Arnim, in her semi-autobiographical book, *Elizabeth in her German Garden* (1898), bemoans this fact with wit and charm. Because of her gender and status (she is married to an aristocrat), hands-on gardening is a luxury she can't afford. 'If I could only dig and plant myself!' she laments. 'How much easier, besides being so fascinating, to make your own holes exactly where you want them and put in your plants exactly as you choose.'

At one point, Elizabeth enjoys a glimpse of horticultural freedom. Evading the eyes of her servants and gardener, she rushes outside, grabs a spade and digs a little patch of ground. She sows a few seeds and hurries back into the house to hide behind a book, acting as if nothing has happened. After her little adventure she concludes that gardening 'is not graceful, and it makes one hot; but it is a blessed sort of work'. Blessed indeed.

In previous decades, Elizabeth von Arnim's middle-class forebears had enjoyed a liberation of sorts. The person who put gardening on the map for Victorian women was English author Jane Loudon. All over Britain, 'ladies' were keen to play a more active role in their gardens, but needed someone to show them how. Loudon came to the rescue with practical, no-nonsense guides. Her bestselling book, *Instructions in Gardening for Ladies* (1840), covered the rudiments of gardening and more – from digging and seed sowing to pruning and propagation. Given the right tools and instruction, Loudon believed women were just as able as men to enjoy gardening. Obvious today, but clearly rather shocking in those days.

Doing things for yourself is part of the appeal of gardening work, especially for those who yearn for a bit of freedom and control in their lives. Elizabeth von Arnim knew that. Jane Loudon gave women the means to do it. 'No lady is likely to become fond of gardening who does not do a great deal with her own hands,' she writes. The same, of course, goes for men and children.

*****

Gardeners are never idle and rarely bored; there are always jobs to be done. Here is my to-do list for this week: clip box, mow lawn, weed drive, prick out seedlings, sort out patio pots (the spring bulbs are now over). I'm not always filled with joy at the prospect of such tasks. Sometimes the pressure to get things done is daunting, especially in the busy spring months. But either the end result or the knowledge that I will get into the process – or both – is enough to get me going.

The pedestrian, repetitive, up-and-down nature of lawn-mowing leaves me cold. Clipping box, though, I find wonderfully immersive and rewarding. I get so wrapped up in it I sometime wonder whether I should have been a hairdresser. All those little nips, all that refining to get the shape just right. Pruning a small piece of topiary is a satisfyingly self-contained piece of work. In less than half an hour, it's done. And what pride at the result! Just look at that neat, bright green ball of loveliness. And it's not just stand-alone perfect. Its newly crisp outline makes everything around it look more attractive – like an inside-out frame to the neighbouring ferns in my border, whose unravelling fronds suddenly come into focus.

Once completed, most gardening jobs produce a spark of satisfaction and tangible results. Some people prefer to spend time in their garden relaxing and sipping wine. There's room for both, of course, but I think the latter is more pleasurable after a good gardening session – and definitely not before, trust me.

This somewhat Protestant view that life that is better lived through productive pursuits – rather than just lounging about – was partly responsible for the growth in Britain's allotments. What better way to keep workers away from the alehouse and other temptations than to occupy them with a patch of land? The idea came to the fore in the late 18th century, when philosophers, social commentators and the gentry started voicing their opinions on the subject. Here is Scottish Enlightenment philosopher David Hume on gardening: 'Men are kept in perpetual occupation and enjoy, as their reward, the occupation itself, as well as those pleasures which are the fruits of their labour. The mind acquires new vigour; enlarges its powers and faculties; and by an assiduity in honest industry, both satisfies its natural appetites, and prevents the growth of unnatural ones' ('Of Refinement in the Arts', 1760).

Preventing the growth of 'unnatural' appetites among workers was a big deal for landowners and industrialists. Let's avoid drunkenness, disorder and – heaven forbid! – revolution, by giving men some land to look after. Honest industry, a kind of imposed good life, equalled virtue. It also meant healthy, happy and grateful employees. When the 'Father of the Railways' George Stephenson provided houses with gardens for his miners in the 1830s, he wanted to foster 'a love of home'. At Merton Abbey, William Morris's textile design and printing factory in Surrey, there was a vegetable garden divided into plots which workers could tend. How wonderful to be able grow your own asparagus (which they did) between shifts. Morris knew how to create a happy and productive work environment. His employees were paid higher than average wages, apprentices slept for free on the premises, and there was even a free library, not to mention ducks waddling around.

It's interesting to note that many allotments and garden plots for workers were intentionally restricted in size. Let's not exhaust the workforce: they need to conserve their energy for the working week. Most allotments also came with sets of rules. You had to pledge to go to church on Sunday and not visit an alehouse on the Sabbath. It was all part of living a virtuous life.

Of course, keeping the working classes away from temptation wasn't the only aim. There were more obvious and pressing reasons, such as the provision of food. Decades of private enclosure acts had led to one-third of England's agricultural land (about 5 million acres/2 million ha) being enclosed by 1845. At the same time, the population was rising sharply. Economists were forecasting mass starvation.

Starting in the late 18th century, something of a restitution took place. Gradually, allotments come to replace the common land that workers had relied on for sustenance. With the Allotment Act 1887, all local authorities were obliged to provide allotments if a request was made. In 1890, a Board of Agriculture census recorded that there were

441,024 allotments in England, 6,410 in Scotland and 7,562 in Wales. By 1914 over a quarter of allotments were in towns and cities, offering relief to factory workers from gruelling labour. Having a little patch of your own was not just a way of ensuring food on your plate; it offered a sense of agency and freedom, and much-needed fresh air.

Access to gardens and a desire to relieve workers from the daily grind and overcrowded, squalid cities were key drivers in the early 20th-century Garden City Movement. Social reformer Sir Ebenezer Howard dreamed of a new semi-urban environment with 'bright homes and gardens' and access to 'fields and parkland'. His manifesto-book, *To-morrow: A Peaceful Path to Real Reform* (1898), led to the foundation of the first garden city, Letchworth, in 1903. Each of the houses and cottages were to have front and back gardens.

You get a feel for these plots – and the ideal gardener – in *The Garden City* (1913) by C. B. Purdom. 'You will not find a house in Garden City without one – a real practical garden, not a mere back-yard …. A garden is irresistible to the man of wholesome mind; … he works his own garden, depending as little as may be upon the professional.' Because, after all, 'to come from the train at night or from one's office or workshop in the town, having left the vexations of affairs behind, to enter one's own quiet garden where tranquillity rests upon the scent of earth and flowers, that is the daily refreshment of every man of Garden City.' As well as refreshment, 'the occupations of the garden provide excellent training for the world and the government of affairs. They add dignity and self-confidence, and cause men to think well of themselves.' Clearly, gardening was a boon to the Garden City man. Not only did it improve his happiness and character, it could even help progress his career.

This garden ideal still resonates today. For many people, having a small back garden where they can escape the 'vexations' of work and stresses of city life is heaven on earth. For those with no gardens, an allotment can serve the same purpose. For me, allotments hold as much magic as private gardens, if not more. I am lucky to have my own garden, but I'm always drawn to these semi-public plots full of character and individuality. Whenever I walk past my local allotments, I slow down and have a good look. All these little parcels of earth invested with such care and attention. Each one a little microcosm. They're rarely perfect – brilliantly reassuring for an untidy gardener like me – and some offer brilliant displays of ingenuity in the use of recycled materials and touches of fun too (one of my local plots has fairy lightbulbs strapped around a wigwam). Often, I have to refrain myself from walking right in, grabbing a fork and getting stuck in. I imagine that's how Elizabeth von Arnim felt.

Some of the challenges we face are very similar to those of our industrial forebears. Many of us live in overcrowded cities. We're tired and overworked. Technology is wearing us down. We crave green space and contact with nature. Some people find it in their garden; others yearn for a plot of their own. Guerrilla gardeners colonize the streets. Those in flats grow window boxes, create indoor jungles out of houseplants, join community gardens.

Working conditions are a lot better (in some parts of the world, at least) than they were 150 years ago. But now we need relief from the new digital revolution. So, when you feel like a small cog in an enormous wheel, when work is turning your brain to mush, when you've had too many virtual meetings, when social media is making you question your own and everyone else's sanity, or you just feel like the world has gone mad: pick up a trowel and get gardening. Your power – and sanity – will be restored. And you might even be more effective at work.

*****

Gardening is exercise with purpose. It's as good for you as many kinds of sport. You burn more calories per minute digging than you do playing badminton or doing yoga or gymnastics. Being an all-round 'sport', gardening has the added bonus of working all the main muscle groups. It gives your heart and lungs a workout. It increases muscle strength and flexibility, boosts your immune system, improves sleep quality, and lowers cholesterol and blood pressure. It may even help increase your life expectancy: exercising in nature rather than indoors stimulates an enzyme known as telomerase, which is believed to help regenerate DNA in our chromosomes and therefore possibly prevent age-related illnesses.

Gardening doesn't always give you as intense a workout as in the gym, but because we're distracted in the garden, we spend longer exercising there than we do inside. We're involved in a process where fitness is not the end result, but a brilliant side-effect.

Sometimes at the weekend, when most people are still asleep, I slip on my gardening boots and walk into the garden. The air is fresh and the day full of potential. Surveying my plot doesn't take long: it's an average-sized rectangle at the back of a 1930s council house. But the ten minutes or so I spend looking round are enough to galvanize me into action. Automatically, I grab a trowel and start attending to some weeds. I imagine I'll spend an hour or so doing a few tasks, but by 11am I'm still out there. I make a coffee and go back into the garden. The day is heating up and I'm spurred on by my early morning achievement and all the little things I need to do to make the garden look good. Before I know it, it's lunch time. The lawn still needs mowing. I want to plant out my cosmos and rearrange the patio pots, and maybe treat myself to a plant from the local nursery. Four o'clock and it's time for a cup of tea and a sit down. I've hardly stopped all day, swept by a wave of small jobs that somehow equate to happiness. I've managed to shed the cares of the week and get a workout.

My hands are dry and tingly from nettle stings, but they'll soon be relieved by a generous helping of hand cream after a long soak in the bath. That evening, as I sit on my bench overlooking the garden, I gloat at my handiwork. The lawn is nice and trim. My freshly weeded cutting garden is packed with floral promise. The borders are starting to fill up and my beloved plume poppy is looking resplendent against the setting sun. It's all so gratifying and pride-inducing. And yes, I have a glass of wine in my hand.

Tomorrow I'll probably feel sore from all the bending and lifting. I don't care. I am restored. This is actual, proper work. None of the screen-based game of email ping-pong, video calls and report-writing that the week is filled with. This is real, salt-of-the-earth work. And – if you'll pardon the pun – gardening work might not pay the bills, but it repays us in spades.

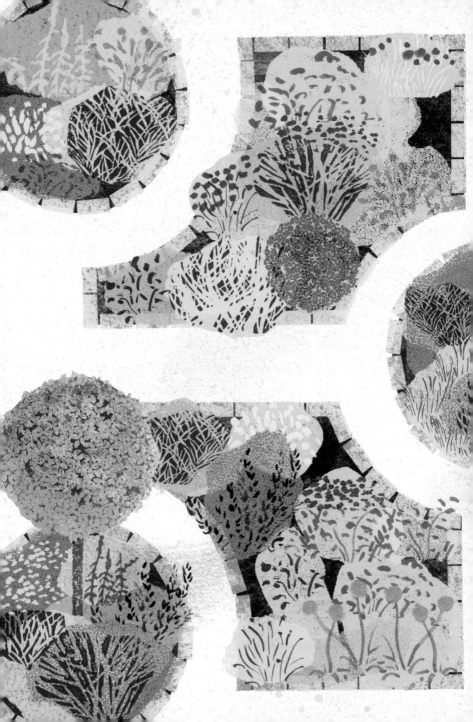

Order

'In the garden or allotment we are king or queen.'

MONTY DON

For many of us, the garden is somewhere we can exert a level of control. It's our own little dominion. We're free to shape it in any way we like. If I want to pave the whole thing, nothing and no-one will stop me. If I want to fill it with vegetables, I can. I call this playing God in the garden. We all do it – it's a big part of gardening's appeal.

The ultimate control-freak garden-maker was the French king, Louis XIV. His garden at Versailles is the epitome of nature moulded to the nth degree. As a symbol of absolute power and the seat of the French court, it helped – along with the equally intimidating palace of Versailles – to keep the aristocracy in check. The garden was not just a work of horticultural art; it was a grand political statement.

Louis XIV's royal gardener André Le Nôtre was responsible for this vast, tightly regimented space. He transformed a royal hunting ground 15 miles (24km) west of Paris into sweeping terraces with pools of water, immaculate lawns, intricate parterres and avenues of razor-sharp hedges punctuated with statues. All this was planned according to the strictest geometry, producing a feeling of complete order and harmony.

Armies of labourers shifted tons of soil to create a hospitable terrain for lawns, evergreens and mature trees, thousands of which were uprooted from nearby woods. Engineers diverted water from rivers and channelled it into the garden's water features. Local villagers were evicted from their homes to provide the required land. People and nature yielded to the command of the god-like figure of Louis XIV, self-named the Sun King after the Greek god Apollo (whose emblem is the sun). Louis was the shining light at the epicentre of France: the star that gave life to all things and could just as easily take it away.

Le Nôtre had studied perspective and the laws of optics. He knew how to shape land to manipulate perception. At Versailles, the Grand Canal initially appears larger than it is: it seems to go on forever – like a huge infinity pool. Just like the king's power, it appears limitless. The principle behind this feat of design – whereby things are made to look different from a certain viewpoint – is called anamorphosis. Another example of this technique is in Holbein's *The Ambassadors* in London's National Gallery. In the painting, a distorted image in the foreground becomes clear only when viewed from a certain angle. The form then reveals itself to be a skull – a clever *memento mori*, reminding us that life is short. Like Le Nôtre, Holbein was able to produce such tricks of the eye thanks to his mastery of perspective.

While much of the garden at Versailles is grand and expansive, it also reveals itself gradually. Avenues leading off from the main avenue tempt you into shady groves enclosed by hedges. These were the setting for small-scale parties and performances, often accompanied by the sound of water gushing from fountains. Like all great garden-makers, Le Nôtre deftly used proportion and perspective, light and shade, surprise and delight. Working closely with Louis XIV, with whom he became friends, he spent the last 30 years of his life refining and extending the garden, while also making his mark on other grand French estates, such as Chantilly and Fontainebleau. Few people realize that he was also responsible for Paris's most famous avenue, the Champs-Élysées.

* * * * *

What does Versailles have to do with your garden? Very little, you might say, but it is relevant in many ways. As I've said, your garden is your own private fiefdom. And, just as with Versailles, the sense of order and harmony you can create there is both visible and symbolic. A neatly trimmed hedge, freshly cut lawn or finely orchestrated border – all are displays of your own power and agency. You have made a mark on the world and created order out of chaos. There's something comforting about this: something which our frail and battered egos – like an egomaniacal king – can cling to for reassurance.

After a day of weeding, clipping and mowing, I like to look at my plot from my French windows. From here I can see the whole garden. In the morning, everything felt like a mess but now order has been restored. The garden has regained a certain clarity and structure, and this is deeply gratifying – not just to the eye, but to the mind.

I used to cast a critical gaze over my neighbour's immaculate plot. He had, as Mirabel Osler put it, 'the antiseptic tidiness that characterizes a well-controlled gardener' (*A Gentle Plea for Chaos*, 1989). Every summer his perfect lawn was fringed with the same bright red geraniums, planted with equidistant precision. His edges and hedges were always neat. It's a wonder they ever had time to grow. His borders flaunted weed-free soil in between the plants. Nothing was ever allowed to wander and mingle. I never understood his way of gardening, but I'm sure all that neatness gave him the same peace of mind and sense of control that I feel after a day of garden tidying.

We may not be despotic kings or queens, but we are all a little bit Mr McGregor. Our approach varies dramatically, of course. Some people resort to weedkiller and harmful slug pellets. I hate the idea and would rather have dandelions in my lawn and watch my dahlias be nibbled. But I'm pretty obsessive when it comes to my patio pots. I spend ages tweaking their arrangement, getting them to appear 'just right'. They mustn't feel too rigid or symmetrical. Rather, they should look like they've occurred naturally, as if they were always meant to look like this, in a pleasing kind of inevitability.

Whether natural or formal or a mix of both, every garden is a designed space that reflects the aims of its creator. The best, I think, are the result of an overarching vision. What do I want from my garden? How do I want it to look and feel? This is the kind of questioning and clarity of intention that will make sure your plot has unity, harmony and that wonderful sense of just-rightness that I was talking about.

Versailles holds within it guiding principles which you can use in your plot. Like Le Nôtre, you can manipulate your space to make it look bigger. Use straight lines to lead the eye and paths to guide the feet; water to add sound or reflect the sky; topiary, plants and pots as rhythm and punctuation; hedges as walls. All this is garden language that doesn't change.

You can be your garden's art director. You can use tricks of the eye to enhance your space and create atmosphere. Focal points can help your garden feel bigger by deepening the sense of perspective. A green climber in a small, shady backyard can give the illusion of greater space. Cool colours, such as blues and light pinks, have a receding effect and will make your garden extend outwards. Hot colours – which pop out – make everything feel closer. Opposing colours (blues and oranges; purples and yellows; red and greens) produce a sense of tension and excitement. Symmetrical elements are calming. Even a small window box can showcase these skills.

I'll admit I'm pretty rubbish at planning. When I started in my garden 20 years ago, apart from wanting it to look 'cottagey', I didn't have much of a plan. I just wanted to grow beautiful flowers. But I knew I needed some sort of evergreen structure – anchors around which the rest of my plot could take shape. I'm glad I decided then to plant a few tiny box shrubs at key points in the garden. They have now grown into large, handsomely rounded specimens. In winter they come to the fore, their reassuring presence like buoys on an empty sea. Heaven forbid they should ever succumb to box caterpillar or blight.

Creating good bones is something garden designers often talk about. Russell Page knew all about this. Self-described as 'the most famous garden designer you have never heard of', he created gardens for the rich and famous in Europe, North and South America and the Middle East. His book, *The Education of a Gardener* (1962), is an account of his lifetime spent gardening. It is now a classic; and what he writes is as inspiring for the amateur gardener as it is for the professional.

He is especially helpful if – like me – you feel you need greater lucidity. He advocates taking a leaf out of the French gardeners' books (I feel Le Nôtre peering over his shoulder): 'The clarity of French planning ... was always helpful to me as discipline for my rather shapeless jungle of a mind, apt to become over-furnished with purely horticultural images and associations.' Hear, hear Russell. That jungle of the mind, that horticultural brain fog can really stop you from seeing the wood for the trees. Simplicity and coherence were his watchwords. 'In making gardens, those which come the nearest to having a sense of unity and inevitability are those in which I have managed not to allow second thoughts or distracting details to blur the original theme.'

One of his most-admired creations is a courtyard at the Frick Collection in New York. It is enjoyed by many because passers-by can see it from the street. Here, in a small space surrounded on three sides by buildings, Page used illusion to create a feeling of spaciousness. On top of one of the walls he added a planter with trees to add height and depth. At ground level, trees of different forms were planted asymmetrically. As he writes in an article in *House & Garden* entitled 'The Shaping of a Garden', this was designed 'to tempt the eye to explore and linger' and create a sense of depth in a shallow garden. Climbers smother one of the walls, which at points seems to vanish in the greenery. A reflective pool of water further expands the space. The garden is a masterpiece of blurred boundaries and – like all his work – of a single-minded, coherent vision.

For all of us muddled, befuddled gardeners, these words by Russell Page should be our mantra: 'Everything that distracts from the idea of a unity must go.' That doesn't mean you have to be minimal and pared back. It's more a case of being clear in what you want to achieve – whether it's a particular plan, atmosphere, colour scheme or style, or a mixture of these. As that other great garden designer, Edwin Lutyens, once wrote: 'A garden scheme should have a backbone – a central idea beautifully phrased.' What's your idea?

*****

Thankfully, nature is more orderly than you might think. And patterns in nature can be as soothing and beautiful as those you try so hard to create in your own plot. It may not feature lines that are dead straight, but the natural world is filled with repetitive shapes. Some of these are known as fractals, which are found both in individual plants and

landscapes (and lots of other natural things, like shells, snowflakes, fungi and clouds). The word 'fractal', coined by mathematician Benoit Mandelbrot in 1975, derives from the Latin *fractus* meaning 'broken'. Mandelbrot defines a fractal as 'a rough or fragmented geometric shape that can be split into parts, each of which is (at least approximately) a reduced-size copy of the whole'. In the garden, you can see fractals in sunflowers, ferns, houseleeks and trees. The more you look, the more you find. A tree repeatedly separates into smaller and smaller branches from the ground up; each branch is a rough copy of the one that comes before.

Designs that repeat at increasingly smaller scales hold our attention by tempting us to follow the pattern to its end. Researchers have shown that we're attracted to fractals because they are easy to process, and they relax the brain. This explains why I can look at my ferns for ages and perhaps also why, when we stare up at a tree canopy, we become mesmerized.

The term 'fascination' has been used to describe this phenomenon. In your garden, you can create your own 'fascination-scape' by using sets of plants of similar shape, and arranging them in groups which interplay and flow and lead the eye.

Despite their apparent jumble and complexity, plant communities such as meadows, hedgerows and grasslands also exhibit patterns. Gardeners who create stylized versions of such habitats are known as Naturalists. Piet Oudolf and Nigel Dunnett are two highly successful exponents of the genre. In Oudolf's book, *Planting: A New Perspective* (2013), co-author Noel Kingsbury (also a Naturalist) explains how, when you stand back and look at a meadow, 'the presence of many thousands of individuals is resolved into something much clearer. This simplicity and clarity amongst complexity gives a sense of coherence ... which enables us to see real beauty in wild plant communities.'

This sense of coherence is often achieved by one or a few species standing out amongst the mass, thanks to their height, colour or form. Picture, for instance, tall spikes of teasels rising above other plants in a summer meadow, or cow parsley and meadow cranesbill along a hedgerow. These 'feature plants' are interlaced with lots of grasses and many other lesser visually prominent species, all densely packed together.

Natural plant communities have inspired many recent and exquisite gardens. At the Lurie Garden in Chicago (2004), Piet Oudolf created a stylized version of an American Midwest prairie, using native plants as the core of his palette. He blended hundreds of varieties, including yarrows, alliums, anemones, sedges and – of course – grasses. Nigel Dunnett's Barbican plantings in London (opened in 2015) feature 'designed plant communities'. As his website explains, 'at any one time it is only two or three plant species that create the main flowering display. But these species are repeated over the whole area, creating maximum impact.'

I like to create a hint of the Naturalist style in my garden by letting tufts of naturally occurring grasses grow tall on the edges of my borders. I realize this is a gardening no-no for many people, but I love the flowing, mingled effect it creates, the blurring between plants. Increasingly too, I let self-seeders pop up where they want. They usually appear in just the right places, offering up their literal 'just-rightness'. Forget-me-nots are especially useful in this respect, filling free spots with a haze of blue and forming a frothy understorey for taller plants.

My relationship with weeds has relaxed too. Who would not welcome a little patch of herb robert? It's basically a small hardy geranium that is unfortunate enough to sit on the wrong side of the horticultural fence. It has the most delicate ferny foliage and light pink flowers, and it pops up in shady places, brightening up the most unpromising nooks and crannies. I've tried growing other things in a shady spot on the side of my house, but to no avail. Herb robert is so happy there, why fight it for the sake of old-fashioned notions of right and wrong? And it's easy to keep under control; it comes out by hand like a dream. Of course, there are weeds you really don't want, but even these can be beautiful. I've accepted that I will never eradicate a tenacious patch of ground elder; now I enjoy its flowering umbels without self-reproach for my lack of control.

Every year my freshly dug veg-and-flower plot becomes dotted with self-seeded poppies. Sometimes I wonder whether I should just leave the ground to its own devices and see what else emerges and how it would look come the summer. For now though, I just leave a few poppies in place and marvel at their brilliant blooms and the beauty of serendipity.

It is this kind of 'spontaneous vegetation' that inspired one of the most visited of naturalistic gardens, New York's High Line. For about 25 years, this abandoned elevated railway line was left in disuse, and

became home to a rich and varied plant life. When the decision was made to create a public garden on the site, Piet Oudolf took as his inspiration this wild, self-seeded landscape. And, as in all his gardens, he celebrated the natural cycles of life and death in nature by letting flowers turn to majestic seedheads come autumn and winter.

Of course, there's a difference between using nature as inspiration and letting nature pop up uninvited in your plot. Both, however, are valid gardening techniques. It's up to you where you draw the line. Sometimes the little plant community that appears out of nowhere looks better than anything you have designed. Natural order is there for the taking if you let it. As we become more ecologically aware and less human-centric, many of us are seeing gardening not as domination but as a harmonious and (mostly happy) collaboration with nature.

Nature

'We all have something in our nature that requires contact with the earth.'

CHARLES DUDLEY WARNER

The American lawyer, editor and writer Charles Dudley Warner is best known for co-authoring a novel with his friend Mark Twain. But he was also a keen gardener. In 1870 he wrote a charming book, *My Summer in a Garden*, in which he describes the trials and delights of his garden. He covers topics close to every gardener's heart, including the source of all horticultural joy: soil.

'The love of dirt is among the earliest of passions, as it is the latest,' he writes. 'There is life in the ground; it goes into the seeds, and it also, when it is stirred up, goes into the man who stirs it. The hot sun on his back as he bends to his shovel and hoe, or contemplatively rakes the warm and fragrant loam, is better than much medicine.'

We now know that what Warner was saying is actually scientifically correct. Sunlight is our main source of vitamin D, essential for healthy bones and teeth. Less well-known is the fact that soil is beneficial to our wellbeing. In 2017, scientists in South Korea discovered that the smell of wet earth, known as geosmin, has a soothing effect on most people. Research has also shown that a bacterium in the soil (*Mycobacterium vaccae*) stimulates the release of serotonin into the brain. When we dig, weed or hoe, we inhale and ingest this natural antidepressant. No wonder our green (or should I say brown?) fingers are drawn to the earth and that children have so much fun playing in the dirt.

Since the 1970s, a theory known as biophilia has suggested that humans have an innate attraction not just to the soil but to the whole of the natural world. The term was first used by American psychoanalyst Erich Fromm, who describes it as 'the passionate love of life and of all that is alive'. American biologist Edward Wilson further developed the concept in his book *Biophilia* (1984). For him, this 'urge to affiliate with other forms of life' has a biological basis. We are genetically tuned to do so. Even more than that, our quality of life relies on it. 'Our existence depends on this propensity, our spirit is woven from it, hopes rise on its currents,' he writes. Without nature, Wilson posited, we become depleted, impoverished.

Biophilia is still a hypothesis, but there is growing scientific evidence that contact with nature – whether through gardening, walking or simply by looking at it – is good for us. Gardening is one of the most immersive and meaningful ways of connecting with the natural world. We see, smell, touch and savour its gifts. We experience its near-miraculous power and endless rhythms. We encounter its fragility and fallibility. And, as gardeners, we enter into an intimate relationship with nature, with give and take on both sides.

Charles Dudley Warner realized that gardening was all about connection. 'In the solitude of garden-labor, one gets into a sort of communion with the vegetable life,' he writes. 'By gardening, I do not mean that insane desire to raise vegetables which some have; but the philosophical occupation of contact with the earth, and companionship with gently growing things and patient processes; that exercise which soothes the spirit, and develops the deltoid muscles.'

*****

We lead hermetic lives, wrapped in a cosy duvet of central heating, double-glazing, air-conditioned buildings, cars and trains. Inside this cocoon, more and more, we engage in a screen-based 'reality': a fake existence that occurs almost entirely in the brain at the expense of the rest of our body and contact with other living beings.

Gardens and gardening help us reconnect with the organic world – the seasons, the weather and the plants and creatures on our doorstep. It's a chance to disengage from our self-centred concerns and wrap ourselves in a bigger and richer blanket. As gardeners, we experience the full extent of what it means to be alive. We feel the cold, the wet and the scorching heat. We get bitten and stung. We smell the roses and the geosmin. We experience the quivering web of life, rekindling a childlike awe at the sight of a flower, frog or seedling.

Right now, in my garden the marjoram is in flower and awash with pollinators: bumblebees, honey bees, hoverflies, tiny mint moths, cabbage whites, meadow browns, tortoiseshell butterflies. It's a cheering sight; a reminder that the world outside teems with life.

But it is more than that. As a gardener, I actually become part of the natural world and its rhythms. All it takes is to sow a seed or plant something and I enter this process. A process which – though I help it along – is much bigger than me, driven by powerful forces. I can't speed it up or slow it down. The seed will grow if I nurture it, but it's not all down to me. It's down to the weather, the seasons, the pull of the moon, the flux of night and day.

There's something comforting about this, and much joy to be had in every season. 'The garden may be different each year – it is, of course – but the swing of the returning seasons is so reassuringly predictable it makes gardening an occupation of utter stability', Mirabel Osler writes in *In the Eye of the Garden* (1993). 'Facing winter the fallen leaf is the first sign of spring.' The fallen leaf is not just a symbol of spring. On the compost heap it transforms into a rich, life-enabling loam. In the garden, even death and decay bring new growth.

The joy of anticipation. The comfort of recurrence. The wonder of renewal. Gardeners know these well. Experienced gardeners are so tuned in to nature's rhythms that they rarely need to consult books or calendars. They just know when to do what. After years of tending their plots, their bodies have internalized this knowledge. Like the garden's resident creatures, they are guided by instinct.

I've not reached this stage in my gardening – and possibly never will – but I do get moments when my body takes over from my brain. It has done something so often that it knows what to do. At points like these, when I unwrap myself from my internal brain activity, I feel a simple connection with the world, as if I were returning to an animal state.

'The reason why gardening will always hold its own is not far to seek,' writes E. T. Cook in *Gardens of England* (1908). 'Nature – the Mother of Gardens – holds in her bountiful hands the inexhaustible gift of life, and horticulture is one of her chosen handmaidens to distribute the blessings which she is able and willing to bestow upon all who will work for them.' Blessings indeed. Right now, Mother Nature is flaunting her generosity in my veg-flower patch. My courgette plant has reached triffid-like proportions. In record time its tentacle-stems have spread onto the lawn like an octopus. Semi-hidden under giant leaves, multiple fruits are swelling larger every day. So much growth and bounty from

one seed. The nasturtiums are creeping with equal vigour, under the dahlias and the last of the peas and broad beans, covering every patch of soil available. Topping it all are the sweet peas. Truly the gift that keeps on giving: the more I pick, the more I get.

Nature's gifts have the quality of a miracle. Gardens are filled with a succession of marvels, each one wrapped in the mystery of creation. Snowdrops pushing their way through the snow, the first crocuses opening in the late winter sun. Every day is a chance to be astonished, as new plants appear, fruits ripen, seed heads crystalize and birds return from faraway lands.

Amazingly, as we open our hearts to nature, we also open ourselves to others. By witnessing the beauty and bounty of the natural world, we become more generous and grateful, as if by osmosis. A study at the University of California, Berkeley, led by psychologist Dacher Keltner in 2003, found that experiencing awe makes us happier, kinder, more ethical and empathetic. What better place to encounter wonder than in the dynamic, always giving, life-filled garden?

*****

Generous gardeners know that their garden isn't all about them. When William Morris built Red House on the outskirts of London in 1860, he was respectful of its environment. He despised builders who 'begin by clearing a site till it is bare as a pavement'. His own plot was home to about 80 mature trees, including fruit trees, oak, ash, holly and hazel, and he was determined to preserve as many as possible.

While Morris resided at Red House, a few of the old apple trees were so close to the building that ripe fruit would occasionally fall through open windows on autumn evenings. Climbers such as jasmine and roses covered the walls, further enhancing the harmony between house and garden, and creating homes for birds and other creatures.

Artist and nature lover – and much else besides – Morris drew his inspiration from flowers, trees and birds, which he transferred to designs for wallpapers, fabrics and rugs. By doing so he brought nature into his home and, of course, those of many others. In his garden he created 'rooms' of rose-entwined wattle, blurring the boundary between inside and out.

From his later home, Kelmscott Manor in Oxfordshire, Morris wrote lyrical descriptions of the natural spectacle on his doorstep.

He was captivated by the ever-changing life of his garden on the edge of the River Thames. Birds held a particular fascination. The garden was 'always filled with song' – with 'robins hopping and singing all about', bullfinches chanting 'a little short song very sweetly' and 'swallows sweeping above the garden boughs towards the house-eaves'.

May Morris, in her biography of her father, writes that he 'noted every turn of a leaf or attachment of stem, watched every bird on the wing with keen alert eye: nothing in the open air escaped him.' Until his final days, William Morris found solace in his gardens. Like Monet, he enjoyed 'garden strolling', and made detailed notes of his observations.

Morris was one of the first great environmentalists. He wanted 'all works of man that we live amongst and handle [to be] in harmony with nature'. Today we understand the benefits of creating a sustainable, wildlife-friendly garden respectful of existing trees and in keeping with its surroundings, soil type, aspect and weather. We realize that we're not just the owners of our plots but also its guardians, and that we have duty of care to its residents.

When the German horticulturalist Willy Lange devised his concept of the 'nature garden' in the early 20th century, he believed that plants and animals should enjoy equal rights to those of the garden owner. It's a wonderful thought – and one that now guides me in my gardening. This larger-than-human perspective makes me see my garden as a mini nature reserve that I can help sustain and enhance. Regardless of the size of our plot, we can all play a part.

American garden designer Benjamin Vogt believes that 'gardens are becoming places of activism'. In his compelling book, *A New Garden Ethic* (2017), he writes: 'Your garden is a protest. It is a place of defiant compassion. It is a space to help sustain wildlife and ecosystem function while providing an aesthetic response that moves you.'

Even though it can offer seclusion, a garden is never disconnected from the rest of the world. Migrating birds fly thousands of miles every year, stopping off for a few days, weeks or months in your garden or neighbourhood. In the coldest days of winter, fieldfares and redwings descend on the UK from continental Europe and Scandinavia in search of insects, fallen fruit and berries. Sometimes they visit my garden, heading straight for the pyracantha and cotoneaster. Happily – and totally by chance – both shrubs are in front of my kitchen window.

The birds' arrival is always a thrilling event. It doesn't happen every year, as they prefer food-rich orchards, fields and hedgerows for their foraging. So, when they do visit my garden, I feel as though I've been bestowed a special honour. Redwings are especially striking, with their creamy yellow stripe above their eye, their red flank and mottled breast. I've now started leaving my neighbour's windfall apples on the lawn for them – it's my attempt to mimic a winter orchard. The resident blackbirds are grateful too.

Of course, it's not just birds that come and go from your garden. A whole array of creatures use it as a café, bed and breakfast, or longer holiday let. Some like the bed and board so much they take up permanent residence – and I'm not just talking about cats and dogs (or teenagers).

Just today, as I was adding yet another pot to my patio, I discovered a toad hidden in a half-empty compost bag. After the initial jolt of surprise, I was filled with glee. Toads are highly sensitive to chemicals, so if they decide to live in your garden, it's a sign that you are creating a welcoming habitat. The other good news is that toads love slugs and snails, devouring up to 10,000 every summer. I can really do with all the help I can get on that front.

Conscious that a bag of compost on a patio may not be the best long-term abode, I carefully moved my new tenant, without disturbing him from his current home, close to my actual compost heap. My hope is he'll be tempted by this food-rich and suitably moist and dark residence. I'm assuming he's a male, because of his small size (male toads are generally a lot smaller than females), but I may be wrong. I checked the bag the next day and he was gone. In his stead were two fat slugs, so he may be back soon.

I will always remember the time when my garden become home to a family of hedgehogs. It was the year my son was born, 2006. It wasn't enough that I had one small baby on my hands. I was blessed with four tiny hoglets too. My two cats didn't know quite what to do when the little hogs came out of hiding every evening. But I was smitten and felt a kindred spirit with mummy hedgehog. Unwittingly, I had created a perfect spot for her to give birth and raise her young. The experience left a mark on me. It made me realize that my garden was a precious space. Because I owned it didn't mean it was divorced from the natural world. In fact, it was wholly part of it: a safe house and feeding ground for a huge array of wildlife.

There are so many ways we can encourage nature into our gardens. Some involve not doing anything. Like not cutting back spent flowers in late summer. Every winter my Japanese anemones offer up a mini feast for a cheerful flock of goldfinches. I love watching their acrobatics as they cling onto the slender stems, pecking at the cotton-like seed heads. The other day I saw a little gathering of them feeding on dandelion seeds on a lawn. Who needs a 'perfect' green sward when you can have a flowery carpet and a bird spectacle to boot?

More and more I see my garden as a backdrop to a natural spectacle, rather than as the main act. Right now, my buddleia is covered in butterflies. Glamorous peacocks hold court over the others, but I favour the more elusive comma. Its gold and black markings remind me of leopard print and its distinctive jagged wings have a charm of their own. When closed it takes on a different appearance altogether: dark brown tones make it appear like a withered leaf, but look closer and you'll spot a little white comma on its underwing.

At times there are so many butterflies on my buddleia it's a job finding a spare flower. I'm tempted to count them, but in the moment I'm so beauty-struck I can't be bothered. Naturalist Richard Mabey did though, and regularly reported seeing 'more than 50 individuals of up to ten species together on a single bush' in his garden.

*****

Even small gardens can harbour a rich variety of wildlife. In 1971, zoologist Dr Jennifer Owen embarked on a mammoth task which no one had ever attempted before. She decided to record all the plants and animals in her garden. Over the next 30 years she counted 2,673 species: 474 plants, 1,997 insects, 138 other invertebrates (spiders, woodlice, slugs) and 64 vertebrates (including 54 birds). She even found a species of tiny wasp new to science. Amazingly her garden played host to 56 per cent of all UK species of bumblebee.

There was nothing special about Owen's garden, apart from possibly her reluctance to use pesticides and to over-prune. It was average-sized and located off a busy commuter road in suburban Leicester. It had a lawn, a small pond, flower and vegetable beds and a few shrubs and trees. In 2010 she published her ground-breaking research in a book, *Wildlife of a Garden: A Thirty-Year Study*. For the first time, there was compelling and thorough scientific evidence demonstrating how important gardens can be in supporting a rich biodiversity.

This scale and length of Owen's research has yet to be repeated, but there is increasing interest in recording the wildlife in gardens. We now know, for instance, that the density of birds in town gardens is six times the average for the UK as a whole.

Things are shifting. As Fergus Garrett, Head Gardener at Great Dixter in East Sussex, says: 'Once regarded as part of the problem, gardens can now be seen as part of the solution.' (*Gardens Illustrated*, Issue 288, 2020.) Recently, Garrett instigated a comprehensive biodiversity audit of the Great Dixter estate, covering its woodlands, pasture, meadows and its famous garden. The results, published in 2020, were astonishing. They showed that the ornamental garden was more biodiverse than all the other areas. As Garrett says, it's 'a prime example of how biodiversity conservation can be integrated into gardening, demonstrating how gardens can play a crucial role in reversing the loss of biodiversity in the UK'. Like Jennifer Owen, the team at Great Dixter don't use herbicides and pesticides. They haven't sprayed for ten years. As a first step to welcoming wildlife into our plots, let's all decide to cut out all harmful chemicals from our gardening.

A garden may always be human-made and therefore artificial, but with a little care and forethought it becomes a nature and wildlife reserve. 'There is nothing more rewarding than plants showing you they are happy by making themselves at home,' Dan Pearson writes in *Natural Selection* (2017). I would add that equally rewarding is seeing birds, hedgehogs, hoverflies and all sorts of other creatures enjoying your garden hotel.

Sanctuary

'The garden is the place
I go for refuge and shelter,
not the house.'

ELIZABETH VON ARNIM

In *Elizabeth and her German Garden* (1898), the eponymous heroine
escapes into the garden whenever she can. 'In the house are duties and
annoyances, but out there blessings count me at every step,' she writes.
Her garden is her sanctuary, where she feels 'protected and at home',
where 'every flower and weed is a friend and every tree a lover. When
I have been vexed I run to them for comfort, and when I have been
angry without just cause, it is there I find absolution.' Her garden
even bestows kindness and forgiveness.

Like all good sanctuaries, Elizabeth's garden is a place apart, divorced
from everyday concerns. In many ways it represents freedom: this is *her*
space where she can – at least for a while – break free from being a wife
and mother. She can read, write, think, be herself. As she says, it feels
more like home than the house.

I think many of us can relate to Elizabeth, especially since the
challenges of lockdown. Trapped in our homes and rendered stir-crazy
from boredom, claustrophobia or intense contact with loved ones,
we turned to our plots, pots, patios, balconies, sheds, windowsills and

greenhouses for simultaneous refuge and escape. In those long weeks and months, we felt the pull of gardening. We turned to the soil for solace, and it provided. And despite being cloistered in our homes, we felt free.

Of course, gardens aren't just a way of escaping 'them indoors' or the confinement of our walls. They're hideaways from the world outside, too. In 1919, Londoners Virginia and Leonard Woolf acquired Monk's House in East Sussex as a country retreat. Here, in splendid isolation, they would write, read, garden, listen to music and walk the South Downs. Significantly, it was the garden that first attracted them to Monk's House. Quaint though it was, the 16th-century cottage wasn't the deciding factor in their purchase. 'The point of it is the garden,' Virginia wrote to a friend, predicting that 'this is going to be the pride of our hearts'. She was right. From the outset, Leonard – a passionate gardener – became obsessed with his plot.

In the 50 years that Leonard lived at Monk's House, the garden acted variously as an asylum from city life, a refuge during the Second World War, a source of comfort after Virginia committed suicide in 1941 and, in his last 25 years, a space to share his gardening passion with his new partner, the artist Trekkie Parsons. Always, the garden was an escape from the outside world, something Leonard actively sought out.

Gardens are often private spaces, protected or enclosed in some way. Throughout history, gardeners have gone to great lengths to enhance this sense of seclusion. So much so that many great gardens are made up of gardens within a garden. Even Versailles – that vast, expansive space – features over a dozen enclosed and secretive groves. Tucked away from the main spectacle, they are little havens, saturated in mystery and out-of-this-world magic.

Harold Nicolson, co-creator of Sissinghurst with his wife Vita Sackville-West, described his plot as 'a succession of privacies'. The garden 'rooms' amount to a 'series of escapes from the world, giving the impression of cumulative escape.' Because of this, Sissinghurst 'has a quality of mellowness, of retirement, of unflaunting dignity.' Anyone who has been lucky enough to enjoy its famous White Garden on a quiet day will know what he means. Theirs was not one sanctuary but a string of them, each with its own atmosphere, each a garden in itself, self-contained and introspective. The vibrant yet homely Cottage Garden, the romantic Rose Garden, the light-suffused Nuttery, the peaceful Herb Garden – all share that same quality of quiet withdrawal.

Thankfully you don't need a garden like Sissinghurst to enjoy this kind of sheltering influence. You don't even need a garden. A balcony or patio will do. The smaller and more restricted the space, the more intimate it is. For me it's about having a nook where you feel no one can reach you. My garden is overlooked and sits cheek by jowl with four others. But there's one spot – overhung by a neighbour's tree – where I feel less exposed. That's where I sit. When the light starts to wane and the daytime noises of children and power tools have stopped, I can sense the garden's comforting bower. Everything is still and quiet. The bats are circling the garden. Like Elizabeth, I feel safe, free of all cares.

*****

Gardens are natural sanctuaries. Often, though not always, they are cut off or at least marked out as separate from the outside world. The word 'garden' provides a clue: it derives from the old German word 'garth', which means 'enclosure'. Other garden-related words and phrases have similar connotations. The term 'paradise garden', for instance, comes from the Persian *pairidaeza*, meaning 'walled-in'.

Paradise gardens go back at least to the time of Persian emperor Cyrus the Great (c. 600–530 bc) and have influenced garden styles throughout the world. In the 6th and 7th centuries, nomadic Arabs created paradise gardens in the middle of the desert. These were lush oases, where water, shade, flowers and fruits offered vital refreshment and shelter to travellers. The most traditional expression of the paradise garden is the *chahar bagh*, or 'four-fold garden'. Here the space was divided into four equal parts by intersecting paths or water channels, with a well, fountain or pavilion at the centre. It's a classic design that occurs in gardens from Iran to India to Andalucía.

The same sense of seclusion is expressed in the medieval *hortus conclusus* ('enclosed garden' in Latin). Typically, it had a central fountain; sometimes it was also divided into quadrants. The garden was closed in by walls, wattle fences or trellis. Tunnelled pathways and arbours occasionally featured, adding to the sense of intimacy.

The *chahar bagh* and *hortus conclusus* were highly emblematic, charged with religious symbolism. In the Islamic tradition, the former represented paradise. As described in the Quran, this was a place of refuge and bounty, where the four rivers of life – of water, honey, milk and wine – would flow. The *hortus conclusus* – closed off and impenetrable – was associated with the Virgin Mary and the central water source, the Fountain of Life, with baptism. As we'll see in Spirit (page 102), gardens have long been linked with religion and notions of heaven.

Whether religious or not, gardens have become loaded with meaning. Perhaps the most relatable is the idea that they bring us peace. When the ancient Greek philosopher Epicurus moved to the outskirts of Athens, he set up a school known as The Garden. It was a community of friends: they lived together, studied together and grew their own food.

At the entrance was this inscription: 'This garden does not whet your appetite; but quenches it. Nor does it make you more thirsty with every drink; it slakes the thirst by a natural cure, a cure that demands no fee.' Fittingly Epicurus thought that peace of mind – or *ataraxia* ('freedom from worry') – was the key to happiness. He found it in his garden sanctuary, away from the disturbances and temptations of city life. This was his 'natural cure'.

Centuries of history have influenced our notions of what gardens represent. Our metaphors are borrowed from the earliest gardens, whether Persian, Greek, medieval or other. Your patio might be where you find *ataraxia*. It might be your 'kingdom of heaven', as Elizabeth von Arnim describes her plot. Your allotment might be where you feel safe. It is your oasis, provider of plenty and protection. And even though it isn't actually enclosed, it is a refuge of sorts and just as valid and comforting as the most secretive *hortus conclusus*.

The idea that your garden is a place of safety and separateness can lie solely in the imagination. As Penelope Hobhouse writes in *The Story of Gardening* (2002): 'Today, for many of us, the garden is still an oasis, a place apart, though the concept may exist as much in the mind as in reality.' Sanctuary can be found in any garden, even when there is no fence, wall, hedge or sheltering tree to speak of.

If you've been to Prospect Cottage in Dungeness, you'll know how it feels to encounter a garden sanctuary without walls. A desolate shingle beach in the shadow of a nuclear power station is where artist and film-maker Derek Jarman chose to create his improbable heaven. A more exposed garden you're unlikely to experience. It's impossible to tell where the garden stops. It just slowly, imperceptibly merges with the landscape. The environment may be barren and bleak – it feels like you've reached the end of the world – but the garden is strangely homely. Perhaps it's to do with the contrast between the boundless sky and brooding power station and the lovingly tended garden of ground-hugging plants and artfully arranged stones and driftwood. At its centre, instead of a well or fountain of life, is a cottage, a source of light and warmth. Its spirit radiates beyond its walls and into the garden.

'There are no walls or fences,' Jarman writes in *Modern Nature*, his moving diary of the years 1989 and 1990. 'My garden's boundaries are the horizon. In this desolate landscape the silence is only broken by the wind, and the gulls squabbling round fishermen bringing in the afternoon catch.' Despite its lack of protection, the garden feels strangely – almost magically – grounded and grounding, rooted in the shingle. It was his refuge, his sanctuary, his paradise. It brought him peace of mind as he quietly battled with AIDS. 'Paradise haunts gardens, and some gardens are paradises. Mine is one of them.'

*****

Jarman left the world behind by moving to a remote coastal headland. His sanctuary, in a way, was Dungeness. He had found somewhere, a landscape, that was virtually cut off from civilization. But in getting away, he got closer to the fundamentals of life. Surrounded by simple and essential things – the sky, the sea, stones, shells, plants, old bits of wood and metal, he was stripped of modern-world contrivances. He had beehives and a herb garden. It was a simple, monastic-like life. 'I can look at one plant for one hour,' he writes. 'This brings me great peace. I stand motionless and stare.'

As much as it can be beautiful or productive, a garden is also a passage somewhere else. As Jarman realized, it opens the door to peace and stillness of mind. Because you feel protected and relaxed, it helps

you transcend your everyday stresses and circumstances, creating
a sanctuary of the mind. Here you will encounter hidden treasures:
a long-lost memory, the idea for your next novel, the solution to
a niggling problem, your life's calling, or just the pleasing and
gratitude-inducing sensation of the sun on your back.

Mirabel Osler condenses this idea when she writes that gardens
'form a small calm eye in a world gone mad'. Truly, gardens are
modern-day oases. We need them now more than ever. The outside
world has insidiously infiltrated our homes. Work, the news, social
media: it's all there 24/7. But your garden – even a terrarium or a few
indoor plants – can protect you from these intrusions. Drop the phone,
close the laptop, switch off the TV. Take your trowel or watering can.
Look at your plants and let them take you away from the chatter.

Sanctuary can be found in the busiest city: your very own *rus in urbe*.
London artist Hester Mallin didn't need a large garden. A balcony on the
23rd floor of a council tower block in Bow, East London, was enough. But
she had big ideas: she wanted a country garden, replete with trees, shrubs,
climbers, fruits, vegetables, herbs, annuals and perennials – the lot. Not
for her a handful of containers to brighten up the place in the summer.
This would be 'a twelve-month garden', beautiful and productive, with
something flowering (and scented) every day of the year.

Mallin managed to grow over a hundred different plants on her
tiny plot. About 230ft (70m) up in the sky, she could step out into her
garden and pick chives and parsley, basil and sage, spring onions, runner
beans and carrots. In winter she enjoyed the scent of *Daphne odora*, the
bright berries of clerodendrum, cotoneaster and callicarpa, and the
cheerful flowers of winter jasmine. Spring brought with it a show of
snowdrops, narcissi, tulips, daffodils, hyacinths and more. And summer,
well, summer was spectacular: 'The containers held a varying symphony

of trailing lobelia, alyssum, carnation, pinks, verbena, geraniums, nasturtium, salvia, stock, antirrhinum, heliotrope, pansy, fuchsia, wallflower, gypsophila, sweet pea and many more.' It's hard to believe she was able to grow so much in such a small and inauspicious plot. But she did. Helicopter pilots would fly past with amazed expressions on their faces when they spotted her garden.

*****

Sometimes other people's gardens can offer just the sanctuary you need. I like to visit gardens that are out of the way or little known as they provide the best opportunity for refuge. But I've also enjoyed quiet times in world-famous gardens. I try to arrive first thing or – better still and if it's a smallish garden – in the last hour of opening. Bad weather also helps. I've seen Sissinghurst in the rain without a soul (apart maybe from Vita's, looking over from her tower).

Once I was scolded for arriving at 5 pm to a garden that closed at 6 pm. The owner, who was at the ticket desk, said to me: 'You realize you've barely an hour to go round.' What she didn't realize is that I'd planned this. I was hoping to have a whole hour in her gorgeous garden all by myself. And I did: everyone was leaving as I arrived. Call me anti-social and smug, but that's surely worth far more than two hours with crowds.

Having someone else's garden to yourself is heaven to me. Along with listening to music, it's my perfect escape. You enter this other world, and all your cares melt away. Because it's not your garden, there's no guilt, just pure pleasure. And the elation you get from experiencing beauty stays with you after your visit.

Garden visiting has sustained me through difficult times. It's been a source of solace and escape during long dark months of depression. It held me together after the break-up of a long-term relationship. Being surrounded by lovingly tended natural beauty makes you feel like things are okay with the world. It rights a wrong – it rebalances your outlook. It gives you hope.

Gardens have always offered opportunities for peace and quiet, but recent initiatives have helped bring out this side of their nature. Established in 1992 by Anglican priest Philip Roderick, the Quiet Garden Movement helps people experience silence in over 300 gardens worldwide. Some are in private houses, others in churches, schools, hospitals and prisons. As the Quiet Garden website explains: 'Time in a Quiet Garden can be helpful for our health and wellbeing, as well as our spiritual journey. Deep restfulness and refreshment within the beauty of creation can often take place, and there will be many opportunities for attentiveness and moments of wonder and transcendence to occur. All these restore body, mind and soul.' This is so true.

In 2016 garden writer Liz Ware set up a similar project called Silent Space. 'There's nothing complicated about a Silent Space,' says its website. 'It's an area of a garden or a park, already enjoyed by the public, that is reserved for silent visiting.' What a wonderful idea. A no-phone, no-camera, no-chat zone. Just you, the garden, and maybe a few other quiet companions.

*****

I'm lucky: I have a shed. Truly it is my ultimate garden sanctuary. A refuge within a refuge. My warm, dusty, spider-webbed cocoon. A shed in the lashing rain is the best: you feel safety and excitement all at once. A shed while you're pricking out seedlings is heaven too – especially if the sun is pouring through the windows and you have a mug of coffee nearby.

Surprisingly, tidying the shed is also wonderful. I hate tidying the house, but I relish the chore in my shed. It's small enough not to be daunting and the feeling of accomplishment far exceeds the effort. And you only have to do it once or twice a year. Chucking empty seed packets, sweeping away a year's worth of dust and dirt, sorting bamboo canes, staking pots ready for seed sowing: it's all thoroughly satisfying. I once toyed with the idea of putting pictures up on the walls – favourite pages from gardening magazines and such like. Then I realized how silly that was. This isn't a shabby chic shepherd's hut. This is a practical, no-nonsense space. And anyway, I love my shed for its rustic bareness, its lack of non-essentials. It's my rough-and-ready zen temple. It clears my mind.

Sometimes I stand in my shed and stare. I stare at the seedlings on the ledge. I stare at the cobwebs. I stare out of the window at the view of

the garden. I stare at the cat luxuriating in the long grass. I'm reminded of the poem 'Leisure' by William Henry Davies, which begins: 'What is this life if, full of care, we have no time to stand and stare?' Gardens give us so many opportunities for contemplation: grab them whenever they come up.

My shed overlooks the whole garden. Abutting the far wall, it gives me a back-to-front view of my plot. I've put an old chair in there so I can look out in comfort. Vantage points are a big deal in gardens and those which offer protection are considered ideal. That's according to the prospect-refuge theory developed by poet and geographer Jay Appleton in *The Experience of Landscape* (1975). He believed that the best sanctuaries combine safety and outlook, and that we have a natural desire for this type of environment. It all goes back to when early humans needed to hide from predators (refuge) but also spot danger and potential prey (prospect). This concept has become a fundamental principle in contemporary garden design and is especially relevant in public spaces. Elements of privacy and enclosure can help create the right feeling of safety and containment, so that visitors can feel secure without feeling trapped. And they can enjoy beautiful prospects too.

In 2019, garden designer Tom Stuart-Smith created a public garden adjacent to the Hepworth Wakefield, an art gallery in West Yorkshire. He turned 1 acre (0.4ha) of exposed grass into a densely planted, naturalistic space punctuated by lawns, curving pathways and wide seating areas, creating a space where people want to linger. The simple device of adding a wall between the garden and the busy road helped transform the garden into a sanctuary. So do the tall grasses and border-hugging hedges. As the plot matures and the trees and shrubs gain in height, this sense of protection will only increase.

It may not be a silent space, but the Hepworth Wakefield Garden is very much an urban oasis. It has become a meeting place for local residents – a place of connection, relaxation, contemplation and inspiration. According to the United Nations Human Settlements Programme, the number of people living in cities is likely to double by 2050. Even fewer people will have private gardens. We're going to need more of these public sanctuaries. In the words of the social reformer Octavia Hill: 'We all want quiet. We all want beauty ... We all need space. Unless we have it, we cannot reach that sense of quiet in which whispers of better things come to us.'

Therapy

'The garden came to me, because I needed it.'

BARNEY BARDSLEY

One of my favourite memoirs – and the best eulogy to gardening as therapy I've ever read – is Barney Bardsley's *A Handful of Earth* (2007). Following her husband Tim's cancer diagnosis, Barney starts gardening. She adds pots and window boxes to her south London flat: flashes of green in a grey world suddenly turned black. In between hospital visits, she pours her heart onto her plants. Tim endures years of cancer treatment. In the midst of all the suffering, Barney gardens. They move to Leeds where they acquire a small garden. 'In time the garden blossomed, even if Tim could not,' she writes. He died a few years later. The book is a moving account of Barney's recovery from loss. Month by month, she describes how she finds hope and healing in her new allotment. 'I began to DIG, with a vengeance, for the future.'

How many of us have found solace in gardening? It has the power to restore faith and repair wounds. Why? For myriad reasons, many of them strangely contradictory. Gardening grounds you in the here and now and stops your mind from racing. Barney recognized its primal, earthy pull: 'The desire to garden felt almost atavistic: as if I were planting myself in the soil, rooting myself in, so that I, at least, would not be swept away by the storm of suffering that had blown into my life.'

I read *A Handful of Earth* while recovering from postnatal depression and anxiety. Everything she wrote rang true. At the height of my illness, I battled with the constant fear of panic attacks. The only way to keep them at bay was to stay busy. It was like being on a treadmill. The garden was full of tasks. It gave me something to focus on, something to get me out of my head. When you're not able to appreciate beauty – or anything really – you can at least do something.

Physical work helped settle my nerves. I remember digging the veg patch in readiness for planting potatoes. I clasped my fork as if my life depended on it. It held me upright and gave me the courage to carry on. As I dug, I felt as if some vital sustaining force was passing from the earth through the fork and into my arms.

Fresh air, exertion, sunlight and purposeful work all seemed to mitigate the anxiety and – for a while at least – dampen my sense of hopelessness. There was something cathartic about tearing out last year's growth, turning the soil, clearing away the weeds. The dark, rich earth spoke of achievement but also of promise. In a few months, there would be a crop of potatoes.

Despite being bound up in the present moment, gardening is a constant looking forwards. It means growth and renewal: a potent reality for depressed minds. 'With its endless cycle of blossoming and withering; its withstanding of cruel winters, of winds and cold, as well as the rush of spring growth and lovely summer profusion, the garden points me forward,' writes Barney. In the words of David Hockney, whatever happens 'spring cannot be cancelled'.

I drank from that well of hope a lot in those dark days. Seed packets meant more than just the thought of plentiful veg and vibrant flowers. They made me fast-forward to a time where I might, just might, enjoy life again. In the midst of despair, they transported me to a brighter future.

Just as it can propel you forwards, gardening can also open doors to the past and help you come to terms with loss. Here is Barney again: 'When I garden, I also search for things no longer mine – times, experiences, feelings, as well as people, from the past. And the strange thing is, I seem to find them.'

Something about the garden's soothing environment, about being surrounded by nature and immersed in simple tasks speaks of simple goodness. Nature is benign and peaceful. It doesn't judge. It is simply there: a safe haven in which you can deal with difficult feelings. As Sigmund Freud writes: 'Flowers are restful to look at. They have neither emotions nor conflicts.'

The psychoanalyst Melanie Klein believed that part of the process of mourning is the ability to regain a sense of goodness in the world. That goodness can come from nature. 'The poet tells us that Nature mourns with the mourner,' she writes. The garden is there, anchoring us, enveloping us, restoring frayed nerves, bringing back memories, rebalancing our outlook.

*****

There is a famous scene in Arthur Miller's *Death of a Salesman*, where the protagonist Willy Loman suddenly decides he needs to plant carrots. His world is falling apart. He has lost everything – his job, his sanity, hope. Instinct tells him that he must put something in the ground. In a rush of panic he starts sowing seeds in the dark of the night. Why does the act of planting sometimes feel like lighting a little beacon of hope?

Maybe this is how George Orwell felt when he decided to up sticks and move to the isle of Jura in the Hebrides. The year was 1946; he had been suffering from tuberculosis for many years. Like Derek Jarman,

Orwell found himself a faraway haven – Orwell called it 'an extremely un-get-at-able place' – and created a garden. Both, in a way, were mourning a loss: the loss of health, the bleak certainty of life curtailed. And Orwell had lost his wife, Eileen, in 1945. Gardening, forever pointing forwards, came to their rescue.

Orwell's domestic diary during his two-and-a-half years on Jura is full of gardening detail. On his second day on the island, he starts 'digging the garden, i.e. breaking in the turf. Back-breaking work'. Two days later, he sows lettuces, radishes, spring onions and cress. Later he plants more vegetables, fruit trees and bushes, all manner of flowers.

This land of tough turf leaves Orwell unfazed. Creating a garden feels like an act of defiance against a seemingly hopeless and barren state of affairs. He is taking on Jura and his own ailing body, as if to say: 'There will be life in this soil and there is life in this old chap yet.' That Orwell wrote *1984* while also creating a garden and looking after his young son Richard is nothing short of miraculous. Thankfully he was not alone: his younger sister Avril and his housekeeper Susan were there too.

'Snowdrops all over the place. A few tulips showing. Some wallflowers still trying to flower.' This is the last entry in Orwell's domestic diary. It is dated 24 December 1948. By then he was confined to his bed, his lung bleeding and about to suffer a major relapse. He died in January 1950.

One of Orwell's aims in life was 'to see what is in front of one's nose' – a fittingly journalistic ambition to capture the everyday, the little details. Through gardening, and through the recording of his garden's development, he was also focusing on the essentials of life. 'Outside my work the thing I care most about is gardening,' he wrote. Writing and gardening provided focus and purpose, and tangible results.

Research has shown that for people suffering from ill-health, stress or depression, gardening can bring a vital a sense of control. They may be unable to change their situation, but they can still affect their surroundings. You can find strength and meaning in the vitality of nature. When you plant a seed, you are boldly asserting that you believe in tomorrow. And, even if tomorrow never comes, in the moment you feel buoyed and that is all that matters.

The other wonderful thing about gardening is that it's a two-way street. When you care for plants, they give you something back. I don't mean beauty or produce, I mean something far more life-sustaining. It took me a while to understand this. Some people – possibly those more naturally nurturing that I am – get it immediately.

I love growing flowers. I used to think it was all about the aesthetics of it: the beauty of a bloom's shape, colour and texture. It still is, but now I'm aware there's something else going on. A sense of deep peace and contentment, a feeling that envelops you, like an aura of gladness. It wasn't an epiphany but a slow realization that by raising and looking after plants I was also looking after myself. Scientists know that being involved in caring activities makes you feel calm and contented. Truly, kindness is a virtuous circle: by changing the world we change ourselves.

*****

Have you ever wondered why you feel at peace after you've been gardening? There are lots of reasons, of course – the sense of achievement, exercise, sunlight, fresh air, contact with the earth – but another explanation is flow.

Flow is something we can all experience when we're immersed in an enjoyable activity. The term was coined by Hungarian-American psychologist Mihály Csíkszentmihályi in 1975. 'The ego falls away. Time flies. Every action, movement, and thought follows inevitably from the previous one, like playing jazz,' is how Csíkszentmihályi describes the sensation of flow. In other words, you're in the zone.

Gardening, like other creative pursuits such as playing the piano or painting, has the power to absorb you entirely, to such an extent that you almost become what you are doing. When this happens, you experience a feeling of at-one-ness with the world. You are no longer trapped in your head, at the mercy of worry or tension. You feel at ease, in sync, as if life were effortlessly fluid – one moment and action naturally flowing into the next. It's like you were always meant to do this.

For flow to take place, the activity should be rewarding and attainable – neither too easy nor too difficult. Gardening is ideal: it provides rhythmic, repetitive activities that involve body and mind. It may take a little time to get into the flow, but once you're there, time starts to become distorted. An hour can feel like ten minutes. And as you become ultra-present, your worries melt away. It's a wonderful feeling: that sense of being in the here and now and nothing else mattering. You feel a sense of ease, purpose and achievement all at once. You are hyper aware in all the right ways; the part of you that is mentally draining and self-critical is turned off. In the end, you feel calm and recharged. Not only is flow deeply restorative, it's also been proven to increase productivity, engagement, creativity and happiness.

A flow state is a bit like a moving meditation. It takes you 'out of your head' via an activity. And the beauty of gardening is that there are always sights, sounds, smells and textures to bring you back to the here and now and away from your thoughts. The English essayist, playwright, politician and landscape gardener Joseph Addison believed that gardens help 'cultivate a virtuous habit of mind'. In an essay in *The Spectator* (1712) he writes: 'A garden is naturally apt to fill the mind with calmness and tranquillity', partly because it features 'innumerable subjects for meditation'.

While we can be immersed in the activity of gardening, a garden can also – by the simple fact of us being in it – provide opportunities for mindful focus or, as psychologist William James describes it, 'involuntary attention'. These are moments when, without realizing it, we become absorbed by something. It could be the amber glint of a backlit leaf, the whiplash tendrils of a pea, or branches gently swaying in the wind. Then, just like William Henry Davies, we simply 'stand and stare'. Such moments of tranquil contemplation can also be deeply restorative – so much so, in fact, that they can help us recover from illness.

In 1984, psychologist Roger Ulrich found that having a view of nature from your hospital bed has beneficial effects. He studied two groups of patients recovering from surgery in a hospital in Pennsylvania. One group had rooms with windows looking onto trees; the other had windows facing a wall. Those in the first group were hospitalized for fewer days, were less anxious and needed fewer doses of painkillers. A later study by the University of Kansas was undertaken with post-operative patients who had flowers by their bedside. The results were similar: less anxiety and less pain medication, as well as lower heart rates and blood pressure.

Even before this type of research was ever undertaken, people realized the healing power of nature on recovering patients. Florence Nightingale experienced it herself. In *Notes on Nursing* (1859), she writes: 'I shall never forget the rapture of fever patients over a bunch of bright-coloured flowers. I remember (in my own case) a nosegay of wild flowers being sent to me, and from that moment recovery becoming more rapid.'

I spent two weeks in hospital after the birth of my son. I had been diagnosed with pre-eclampsia and he was born premature. The whole experience was terrifying. He was tiny and needed lots of tests. My blood pressure was critically high – it was 'teetering on the edge', as one doctor helpfully informed me. I barely slept for the whole time I was in hospital, scared for his life and mine. None of this was helped by the sterile hospital environment. There was not a hint of nature.

I remember the swell of tears when I came home to see my garden in its midsummer bloom. It was indeed a rapture of sorts. Having been starved of aesthetic nourishment, I was hit by the overwhelming beauty of it all. The flowers were so vibrant and jewel-like. Already I knew something wasn't right. It didn't feel like relief; it was more like a tiny spark of joy in my shattered, post-traumatic state. It was I who was teetering on the edge. The full extent of what was happening to me – deep depression, panic-inducing derealization – took just a few days to unfold. Would I have suffered from anxiety and depression had my experience in hospital been different? I will never know. But one thing I do know: nature heals. Gardens and gardening especially so.

*****

This knowledge isn't new. Gardening has been used in mental healthcare for over 200 years. Gardens may not be the first thing you associate with what were then called lunatic asylums. Many of them were insalubrious places where chains, handcuffs and straitjackets were commonly used as restraints, and treatments ranged from beatings to soaking patients in freezing water. But in 1796 William Tuke, a Quaker from Northern England, founded a new type of institution for the mentally ill. Designed for about 30 patients, the York Retreat was a comfortable and airy country house where people could engage in a combination of manual work and leisure. The building was surrounded by nature, with opportunities for walks in beautiful countryside as well as gardening and farming work. The Retreat – which still runs today – became a model for a new kind of 'moral' mental health treatment.

By the 1840s, people had come to realize that gardening could play a key part in the recuperative process. Outdoor work was actively encouraged for those patients who were physically and mentally fit enough. When Dr John Conolly started working at Middlesex County Asylum – then the largest asylum in England – in 1839, he abolished all mechanical restraints, following his belief in the 'mild and human treatment of the insane'. By 1847, he writes of the effects of gardening on the patients there: 'The cultivation of the gardens, and of the ground called the farm, as well as of the extensive ornamental ground in front of the asylum, is entirely effected by the labour of numerous male patients, superintended by gardeners, or by steady workmen. The cheerfulness with which their work is performed, and the satisfaction with which, at stated hours, they assemble for their allowance of beer, sufficiently attest that calming and remedial influences are thus exercised.'

Similar results were witnessed by Thomas Prichard at the private Abington Abbey Retreat near Northampton, in 1860: 'The care of the gardens being, in many instances entrusted to patients, serves as a double purpose – of affording wholesome occupation, and of promoting a tranquil and cheerful tone of thought. The operations of husbandry are largely carried out upon the asylum farm, and many acres of ground are profitably cultivated, both in an economical point of view and as a remedial and curative process.'

Nowadays, a growing body of research tells us that green activities – such as gardening and farming-related work – are beneficial in treating mental-health disorders. Mental-health charities, such as Thrive in the UK, use plants and gardens as a means of improving both psychological and physical health, helping people recover from or manage a wide range of conditions, from anxiety and depression to physical and learning disabilities.

But gardening is also beneficial to the mental health of people who aren't suffering from acute symptoms. In 2002, research undertaken in Sweden showed that the more people garden, the fewer incidents of stress they suffer. Gardening can help prevent us from developing mental-health issues, simultaneously boosting mood and self-esteem and reducing stress and anxiety. In a nutshell, gardening cultivates wellbeing.

*****

Many gardeners know very well the sanity-restoring virtues of gardening; they don't need to be told. Sometimes though, I need to remind myself,

because it's easy for other things to take over. A busy or stressful week, time swallowed up by chores, or a stretch of bad weather can make me feel like I'm neglecting my plot. At times like these it's easy to succumb to gardener's guilt.

It's late November and it's been raining for what feels like weeks. Outside it is damp and cold and I've been focusing on other things, wrapped up in indoor stuff. I tell myself I should be cutting back shrubs, mulching the borders and raking the leaves. I should, but things have conspired against me. If I'm not careful, the garden will become my nemesis, its near state of wilderness an ever-present reminder of my failings. But no. The garden is my friend, and friends are patient and forgiving. They understand.

As I write at my desk – aka the kitchen table – I notice through the window an unfamiliar bird flitting past. I stop staring at the computer screen and try to make out what it is. Its tiny shape alights on the patio table for a few seconds, enough for me to make out it's a firecrest. A firecrest! A tiny ball of cuteness, barely bigger than a conker. I wait a little longer to see if he returns. Moments later he does, and he's brought a friend. The pair dart from table to shrub and back again in a skittish little dance. This reminds me it's time to stock the birdfeeders. I hunt out last year's supply of fat balls and nuts. There's just enough to get me started for the winter. I'll soon be scattering apples on the lawn for the redwings and fieldfares.

This chance sighting prompts me back into the garden. Right now, all I have time for is this simple act of bird-kindness, but something in me has been stirred and a chain of thought set in motion. In my mind I start planning my weekend with new-found relish. I will go out there – rain or shine – and do some pruning. I might even tackle the hedge, and I will definitely plant those tulip bulbs. Before long, I will be in full flow.

Growth

'A garden is a grand teacher. It teaches patience and careful watchfulness; it teaches industry and thrift; above all it teaches entire trust.'

GERTRUDE JEKYLL

Gertrude Jekyll wrote these words in the introduction to her first book, *Wood and Garden*, in 1899. By then her career as a garden designer was flourishing, but Jekyll didn't stop gardening. She was anything but an armchair gardener. 'I have lived among outdoor flowers for many years, and have not spared myself in the way of actual labour,' she writes, also in *Wood and Garden*. Tellingly, the book's subtitle is *Notes and Thoughts, Practical and Critical, of a Working Amateur* and its focus is her own garden at Munstead Wood in Surrey, which she designed and developed.

You may have come across the painting of Gertrude Jekyll's black boots. Sir William Nicholson painted them in 1920, when Jekyll was 76. The story goes that he produced the picture while waiting to paint her portrait (she would only sit for him after dusk, apparently). To fill his time, Nicholson reproduced Jekyll's boots, capturing something of her down-to-earth character. The sturdy, well-worn footwear reveals her to be a grafter: the toes are coming away from the soles, suggesting hours of use. Jekyll was still wearing the same much-repaired boots at the time of her death in 1932. You can see them, along with other Jekyll-related items, at Godalming Museum in Surrey.

As is obvious from the introductory quote, Jekyll realized that gardening develops more than just an understanding of plants. She knew from experience that when we grow a garden, we also grow ourselves. We grow in character and self-awareness. We learn to be patient and resilient and accepting of change. We become more appreciative of the little things. All this thanks to our interaction with nature: a unique to-ing and fro-ing of engagement, an accumulation of experiences that slowly builds up to make us better people. As gardeners, we become pupils, not just of horticulture, but of life.

Perhaps the most wonderful thing about gardening is the least obvious: what it does to us while we're not watching. Jekyll admits that, for her, 'the lesson I have learned most thoroughly is, never to say "I know" – there is so infinitely much to learn.' There's no doubt that gardening makes us humble. 'Nature is such a subtle chemist that one never knows what she is about, or what surprises she may have in store for us,' she writes.

Working with nature is a constant and salutary reminder that as humans we're never fully in charge. As you let go of expectations of everything always going your way, you open yourself to change and even revelation, not only in the garden but in yourself. The experience is richer for being less predictable. When you relinquish complete control, you become more open-minded and adventurous, creating opportunities for delight, wonder and even love. Gardening is an ever-enriching spiral. It can change the way you see the world forever.

*****

I started gardening in my early twenties when I moved into a tiny rented cottage with an even tinier backyard. My 'plot' was about the size of a double bed, accessible only from the downstairs bathroom. This unfortunate situation was made worse by the fact that the yard barely got any sun. It was a dark, damp spot enclosed by mossy walls, but it was mine and I was determined to make something of it.

Excited by my new space, I bought plants and seeds I'd always wanted to grow – sweet peas, tomatoes, a rose, lavender – in the vain hope they would thrive. I tended the seeds on my sunny upstairs windowsill. When they were ready, I moved the seedlings into the yard. They failed, naturally. The tomatoes didn't fruit. The sweet peas made their way towards what little sunlight they could find, growing leggy and never quite making it. The rose slowly withered.

For all my initial disappointment, I remained undefeated. Deep down I knew my attempts were wildly optimistic, but I was compelled to try anyway. Maybe I wanted to see if I could cheat nature. I learned my lesson, and found out that the 'right plant, right place' maxim really is the foundation of all successful gardening. And then I discovered the world of ferns and ivies and filled my yard with these often-underrated shade-loving, easy-going beauties.

We don't make the rules, nature makes them. My first lesson in gardening was straight out of a Rolling Stones hit. In gardening, as in life, you can't always get what you want. Instead, I made something unexpected and beautiful with different plants. As Mirabel Osler says: 'To garden you have to keep an open mind.' My gardening mind has been open ever since.

*****

My unexpected optimism in the face of horticultural failure has remained a constant. The more I garden, the more I am accepting of setbacks, and something of this philosophical attitude has transposed itself into my non-gardening life.

Nature is unpredictable, of that we can be sure. As much as you try to understand what plants like and how best to grow them, your expectations won't always be met. What looks great on paper or in a catalogue can fail through no fault of your own. I've found that disappointment in the garden not only encourages a more accepting outlook, but can actually spur me on, inspiring curiosity and new approaches. After all, much gardening is trial and error.

One of my favourite horticultural experimenters is Ellen Willmott. She spent all her money on gardening, developing a passion and renown for trialling and hybridizing plants. She raised seeds and cuttings sent from

friends and plant-hunters all over the world, growing them in different soils and conditions. Her work was so important and pioneering that she shared it with experts, including those at Kew Gardens. Experimentation fascinated her so much that one year she tried every known variety of potato to find out which would be the best suited to her garden at Warley Place in Essex.

Not content with receiving horticultural gifts in the post, Willmott would come home with cuttings whenever she visited a garden. In an act of playful restitution, she would secretly scatter seeds in other people's gardens. Her favourite plant for this little venture was *Eryngium giganteum*. This thistle-like plant, now fittingly known as Miss Willmott's ghost, is bold and graceful in equal measure – qualities I like to associate with Willmott herself, along with a certain prickliness of character.

A gardening friend recently admitted sprinkling hollyhock seeds along the narrow back streets of Woodstock in Oxfordshire when he used to live there. In the summer you can see the fruits of his beneficence. I'm tempted to start my own seedy errands in my village. Like guerrilla gardeners, I will work under cover of darkness. My pockets filled with sunflower seeds, I will prowl the streets in search of patches of soil, trowel at the ready. Come late spring I may be rewarded with a few healthy shoots. How wonderful it would be to see children's beaming faces as they discover sunflowers popping up everywhere.

Ellen Willmott is the perfect embodiment of an adventurous approach to gardening, where 'failure' is just a necessary stepping stone to success. Every gardener has something of her in them: that spark that makes you want to try something new every year. Even if it's just a few seeds. And even if it's not in your garden.

*****

As gardeners, we're constantly reminded that plants come and go. Annuals come full circle in a less than a year. Longer-lasting plants have their own lifespans too, just like animals. With every season that goes by, you learn to look forward and not dwell on losses. Small sorrows in the garden can help you better deal with grief, reminding you that nothing lasts forever but also, crucially, that life goes on.

And by welcoming impermanence, we're better able to appreciate the present. We can't freeze time, and neither should we try to, for there is joy in the here and now, in the ever-unfolding moment where we can notice change and appreciate beauty. Sometimes this noticing can feel like a little epiphany. It happened as I was raking the leaves the other day. As I got lost in the activity, I felt a comforting swirl of sensations. The earthy smell of damp leaves, the soothing sound of the rake scratching the lawn, the welcome mildness of the air: all combined to create a feeling of warmth and thankfulness. Maybe it's part of growing old – that you find gladness in the little things – but I do believe gardening has helped develop my gratitude muscles. I have become more open to awe. As I've grown inside, my garden has grown in its potential for wonder.

Gardeners are, on the whole, an optimistic bunch. We're (mostly) undaunted by challenge, undeterred by losses and always looking forwards. Why? Because what spurs us on is the thought of growth. We want to generate and nurture life and, after a few years of gardening, we develop faith in our plots and in ourselves.

When I moved into my current home in my late twenties, what should have been a garden was more of a builder's yard, full of accumulated debris. Under the brambles, grasses and assorted weeds were bricks, random bits of metal, broken pots, old toys. Clearing and levelling the ground was a hard, long slog but I got there. For the first time in my life, I felt strong. I discovered I rather liked physical labour. It's amazing what you can achieve when you have vision, and gardeners are natural visionaries. We plot our plots, and with patience and hard graft, we create a haven. As we look after this haven, we nurture positive character traits such as patience, humility and diligence.

Being a mostly silent and solitary pursuit, gardening also encourages reflection. Mirabel Osler nails it when she writes: 'The garden and I have a relationship which means that the longer it goes on the more I surround myself with mental space and, should I want it, self-discovery' (*In the Eye of the Garden*, 1993). If you'll excuse the pun, a garden is fertile ground for the mind. It gives you time and space to consider things more deeply and at a slower pace. It prompts ideas and solutions, and can open doors to parts of yourself you may not be aware of.

Gardening might provide you with the only opportunity for a proper, unencumbered conversation with yourself.

You are in the middle of doing some repetitive task, like pruning, and suddenly a thought reveals itself to you with absolute clarity. Gardening has the power to provoke such sparks of revelation and self-awareness. At times my garden acts like a kind of mirror. For me, this usually happens in the midst of doing something I do on an annual basis, like preparing the veg patch for the new season. Every year that goes by adds something new to the experience, and in the moment you get a kind of slice of life – a bit like strata with its different layers of rock – that shows you how you've changed from one year to the next. Annual gardening rituals can be incredibly revealing.

Every garden is unique and so is every gardener. Your gardening journey is your own, but I'm willing to bet it's a rich and transformative one.

Spirit

'One is nearer to God's heart in a garden, Than anywhere else on earth.'

DOROTHY FRANCES GURNEY

The Lord God planted a garden
In the first white days of the world,
And He set there an angel warden
In a garment of light enfurled.

So near to the peace of Heaven,
That the hawk might nest with the wren,
For there in the cool of the even,
God walked with the first of men.

And I dream that these garden-closes
With their shade and their sun-flecked sod
And their lilies and bowers of roses,
Were laid by the hand of God.

The kiss of the sun for pardon,
The song of the birds for mirth,

One is nearer God's heart in a garden,
Than anywhere else on earth.

For He broke it for us in a garden
Under the olive-trees
Where the angel of strength was the warden
And the soul of the world found ease.

Poet and hymn writer Dorothy Frances Gurney penned the poem, 'God's Garden', inspired by her deep Christian faith. Why is it relevant to this chapter? Because for centuries gardens have been imbued with religious and spiritual meaning. It's a powerful legacy that still affects us, even though we may not realize it.

Dorothy Frances Gurney is referring to the Bible story in Genesis in which God plants Eden, the first garden. As she writes so beautifully, it's a place filled with light, mirth and ease. Humans, animals and plants live in harmony, their souls are at peace; they feel close to God's heart. This is the perfect garden, before Adam and Eve's fall from grace.

For centuries gardens were designed as sacred spaces; worldly reflections of paradise, that eternal, idealized garden. The way we see, experience and even design our gardens has been influenced by cultural and religious concepts that go back to ancient history. The unreachable yet covetable Eden – a blessed place of peace, harmony and spiritual enlightenment – has become an unwritten, often unconscious, aspiration for many gardeners.

And thus gardens are a lot more than just beautiful or productive plots. They can help us transcend the physical world and connect us with the numinous. Truly, gardens are thresholds to another world. They open doors to the metaphysical.

I don't follow any religion, but I do find myself feeling more in touch with my spiritual self when I'm in a garden or in nature. Sometimes the light, the birds, bees, flowers and trees conspire to produce an atmosphere so glorious that I can't help but feel spiritually uplifted. It's as if angels really did exist.

*****

Religious imagery abounds in ancient gardens. The temple gardens of Ancient Egypt featured lakes representing the sacred waters of creation. Around them were plants filled with meaning: date palms denoted the sun god Ra; mandrakes referred to the goddess of love, Hathor; the lotus signified spiritual rebirth. Grouped together around the source of all life, this lush greenery symbolized the original garden from the beginning of the world – what the Ancient Egyptians called *Zep Tepi* (the First Time).

As I mentioned on page 69, Islamic paradise gardens were a foretaste of heaven. Here, too, water was a potent symbol: a reflection – both literal and metaphysical – of the heavens. And here plants also carried religious connotations, inspired by descriptions of heaven (Jannah) in the Quran. Oranges symbolized life. Morello cherries represented the soul. Cypress trees meant both death and eternal life. The Islamic garden was designed as a place of prayer and contemplation, where you could find peace and spiritual enlightenment, exactly as you would when reaching heaven, the eternal garden.

Plants in medieval Christian gardens embodied divine qualities. The white rose and lily signified the Virgin Mary's purity. Violets, because they grow close the ground, suggested her humility. Evergreen plants denoted immortality. The vine represented Jesus Christ, its branches his followers and its grapes the vital life force. Such characteristics were thought to reside in the plant, expressed through its leaf, flower, fruit or manner of growth. In a very similar way, medieval herbalism was based on the notion that a plant's healing power related to its physical attributes, in what was known as the doctrine of signatures. The idea was that God had marked plants with their own signature: a distinctive feature resembling a part of the body, showing what they could treat. Lungwort was used for pulmonary infections because the white spots on its leaves looked like those on sick lungs. With its flower resembling an eye, eyebright was added to tinctures to treat eye infections.

Throughout the pre-Renaissance world, and in many places and cultures beyond it, nature was not just a physical thing you encountered through your senses. Plants and natural places, such as lakes and rivers, were – as it were – ensouled. In Ancient Greece, every plant had its own spirit: *anthousai* resided in flowers; *hamadryads* and *dryads* lived in trees.

For the followers of Shinto, Japan's second largest religion after Buddhism, nature is alive with millions of spirits known as *kami*. To them the visible world (*kenkai*) and the invisible world (*yukai*) are not separate entities: nature is at once sacred and material. Similarly, animism – followed by many indigenous peoples and thought to be one of the earliest forms of religion – states that everything, be it animal, vegetable, mineral or man-made, has its own spiritual essence. Looked at from this perspective, it's easy to see how gardens have been perceived as sacred.

*****

While virtue-invested plants connected you with God or the spirits, and could even make you feel better, so too could a plain rectangle of grass, in the form of the cloister garth or yard. David Manning and Martin Palmer, authors of *Sacred Gardens* (2000), reckon that: 'The very simplicity and emptiness at the heart of the garth reflected the ultimate aim of contemplation, to move beyond the material, beyond words, beyond self into ... the Divine Emptiness.' The same can be said of water in the garden. Water calms and captivates, and can open doors to a higher state of awareness. Even the smallest feature will do. A container filled with water can act as a mirror to the soul or a window into a deeply contemplative state.

In the Chinese Taoist tradition, gardens were designed to help you reach a state of 'no mind' or pure consciousness. Based on the principle of Yin and Yang, the two elemental and contradictory forces, emptiness was considered just as essential in the garden as was generous planting. At the core of the Taoist garden is an emptiness, sometimes expressed as a lake or pond, a small hill, or a just a space outlined by plants. The idea was that at the heart of everything is nothing.

Zen Buddhist gardens take the notion of 'less is more' to extremes. In just a few elements, they aim to capture the essence of the world. Raked sand or gravel symbolizes water; the rocks or stones are islands. But vertical rocks can also denote heaven and horizontal ones the earth. A diagonal rock linking the two is said to represent humanity. White sand means purity of thought. Aids to meditation, Zen gardens are designed to help you reach a state known as *samatha* or mind-calmness. The act of raking the sand can be part of the meditative process, as is the setting of stones, representing the setting of one's thoughts onto a blank canvas.

The Gardens of Japan (1928) by Jirō Harada, quotes the words of Japanese scholar Okakura Kakuzō in which he describes a garden designed to evoke 'the solitude of the soul still lingering amid shadowy dreams of the past, yet bathing in the sweet unconsciousness of a mellow spiritual light, and yearning for the freedom that lay in the expanse beyond'. I can't think of a more poetic way to evoke a spiritual garden awakening.

And here is metaphysical poet Andrew Marvell waxing lyrical about how gardens can bring about transcendence of mind, in these two stanzas from his poem 'The Garden' (1681):

> Meanwhile the mind, from pleasure less,
> Withdraws into its happiness;
> The mind, that ocean where each kind
> Does straight its own resemblance find,
> Yet it creates, transcending these,
> Far other worlds, and other seas;
> Annihilating all that's made
> To a green thought in a green shade.
>
> Here at the fountain's sliding foot,
> Or at some fruit tree's mossy root,
> Casting the body's vest aside,
> My soul into the boughs does glide;
> There like a bird it sits and sings,
> Then whets, and combs its silver wings;
> And, till prepar'd for longer flight,
> Waves in its plumes the various light.

Truly, gardens are magical, Narnia-esque places. They open up possibilities for other worlds and other thoughts, all the while making us look within.

*****

Not all gardens are blessed with this kind of magic. I can think of lots of well-known ones which aren't. They might be filled with beautiful flowers, have immaculate lawns and great bones, but they lack spirit and atmosphere. Quite possibly they are unloved, looked after by staff who go home to their own cherished plots.

Or maybe these gardens don't reflect their spirit of place – that sense of being inspired by, in sync with, their environment. Here, too, we feel the influence of the ancients: the phrase 'spirit of place' comes from the Roman *genius loci* and was taken up by 18th-century landscape gardeners as a guiding principle. It all started around 1731, when the poet Alexander Pope urged gardeners to 'consult the genius of the place'. Here are his famous lines from 'Epistle IV, to Richard Boyle, Earl of Burlington':

> *Consult the Genius of the Place in all;*
> *That tells the Waters to rise, or fall;*
> *Or helps th' ambitious Hill the Heav'ns to scale,*
> *Or scoops in circling Theatres the Vale;*
> *Calls in the Country, catches opening Glades,*
> *Joins willing Woods, and varies Shades from Shades,*
> *Now breaks, or now directs, th' intending Lines;*
> *Paints as you plant, and, as you work, Designs.*

In other words: gardens, landscapes, even buildings should be inspired by what's already there – the topography, the plants, the light, the shade. William Kent, gardener to the Earl of Burlington, to whom the poem is addressed, followed this advice to the letter, creating nature-inspired arcadias at Chiswick House, Burlington's home in London; Stowe in Buckinghamshire; and Rousham in Oxfordshire.

Rousham is Kent's best-preserved and most beguiling creation. I'm lucky to live nearby, and the more I visit the more I fall under its spell. Sinuous paths take you down into a wondrous world of surprise and mystery. Kent's creation is an exquisite game of contrasts: of light and shade, intimate spaces and open vistas, twists and unexpected turns, wilderness and refined art. There are venerable trees, perfectly placed sculptures, small buildings that nestle under trees, eyecatchers in the far distance. And there is water too: in the form of the snaking River Cherwell below, but also – like a diminutive echo – in the glistening rill that runs through light-suffused woodland to a dipping pool. Coming across it feels like a mini revelation, almost as thrilling as meeting the figure of Pan overlooking a larger stretch of water. Half-man, half-goat, in Greek mythology he was the god of wild nature. The Romans, who knew him as *faunas*, associated him with enchanted woods. Truly, Rousham is enchanted. Sometimes it feels like I've stumbled through the wardrobe and reached Narnia, and here is Mr Tumnus greeting me. One day I will visit in the snow and the magic will be complete.

*****

The best gardens possess an atmosphere that transcends reality, opening a door into the invisible. Jeremy Naydler, author of *Gardening as a Sacred Art* (2011), calls them 'mediators of the divine'. For him, Monet's Giverny is a perfect example. Why? Partly because Monet was deeply in tune with nature. He would spend hours contemplating it, allowing himself to notice its subtle, ever-changing moods. Guided by this deep awareness, he created a garden that was so full of 'aliveness and beauty' that – according to Naydler – 'we find ourselves relating not just *to this particular* garden but also to a greater spiritual presence pervading its atmosphere: Nature as such, vibrant, creative and nurturing.'

Monet was obsessed with Giverny, in thrall to its elusive magic, especially his water garden. Here, in this ethereal world, weeping willows

kiss the water's edge, lilies hover over fathomless waters and wisterias melt over bridges. Like Japanese stroll gardens, the meandering paths invite you to slow down, breathe in the atmosphere, and feel spiritually elevated. In the water garden and the paintings it inspired, water, land and sky merge into one, bound by an all-enveloping light.

Giverny is so much more than what the eye can see; there is another dimension to it. Art critic Octave Mirbeau wrote that Monet 'reveals the impalpable, the ungraspable in nature ... its soul, the thoughts of its mind and the beating of its heart.' In his paintings and his garden, Monet crystalizes the intangible.

Any garden – even the humblest plot – has the potential to move you in this way. It's about having the right intention and attention. How does your garden make you feel? Does it make your heart sing? Does it feel like a space apart, but also in tune with its environment?

Have you ever been in garden and felt lighter, buoyed by its atmosphere? And then does everything in the world not feel right? As though you are in touch with everything meaningful and true, almost like you've reached paradise? Call it enlightenment, no mind or divine realization: heaven is right here in the garden.

If you ever find yourself wondering whether you're gardening in the right way, think of these words by William Robinson: 'A garden should be a living thing: its life not only fair in form and lovely in colour, but in its breath and essence coming from the Divine.' If we approach gardening with a sense of wonder and loving kindness towards our plot and plants – like the ancients did – we can create a garden that sings and is full of atmosphere. Just like Monet and William Kent, we can make magic.

*****

Instead of visiting a temple, mosque or church at the weekend, many of us turn to our plots. Working the soil, nurturing plants and watching them grow is a bit like religious devotion. The little rituals and annual celebrations, the regular contact with the essentials of life – earth, water, sunshine, growth – conspire to make us feel spiritually enriched. Even though it may not be a religious experience, it feeds the soul.

St Benedict, whose Rule became an influential guide for how to live in a monastic community, believed that the life of the spirit should be grounded in a close relationship with the earth. Still today, gardening is a key part of many religious communities.

In our own lives, gardening can be more than just a hobby. It can become an essential part of our spiritual life. And what we create in the process – whether it's a flower-filled patio or an abundant allotment – can feel like paradise regained.

Love

'Often I hear people say: "How do you make your plants flourish like this? ... What is your secret?" And I answer with one word, "Love".'

CELIA THAXTER

I mentioned Celia Thaxter in Chapter 1. In *An Island Garden* (1894), she describes how she creates a cutting garden on the island of Appledore, off the coast of Maine. But her book is more than a straightforward how-to guide. It's a hymn to the gardening life, filled with joy and – yes – love.

Thaxter worships her tiny plot, adores her 'dear flowers' and is wonderstruck at the dormant miracles that are seeds. 'Take the Poppy seed, for instance,' she writes. 'It lies in your palm the merest atom of matter, hardly visible, a speck, a pin's point in bulk, but within it is imprisoned a spirit of beauty ineffable, which will break its bonds and emerge from the dark ground and blossom in a splendor so dazzling as to baffle all powers of description.'

Thaxter believes she was born a 'lover of flowers'. This is no superficial thing, no mere aesthetic leaning. As she says, it is a real love worthy of its name, 'capable of the dignity of sacrifice, great enough to bear discomfort of body and disappointment of spirit, strong enough to fight a thousand enemies'. This predisposition means that, given a patch of ground, seeds and a few tools, the lover of flowers will – almost inevitably and whatever the circumstances – create a garden of great charm, to which they will devote their heart and soul.

Are all gardeners not the same? Despite challenges that come our way – rampant weeds, pests and diseases, destructive weather – our love of plants and gardening means we carry on regardless. All because we care. Maybe, as Thaxter believes, a gardener's love is inbuilt. Whether or not it is, one thing is certain: gardening is an act of love. It brings out the best in us. And this impulse to grow and nurture plants spills us beyond our gardens, bringing joy – and much else besides – to ourselves and others.

Creating and maintaining a garden is like a relationship. It needs attention and constancy. It is built on respect and kindness. As the bond deepens, you begin to know when to offer support and intervene, and when you don't need to. You start to notice and appreciate quirks you hadn't seen before. A few may niggle at you, but many more make you glad. Eventually, you become almost intuitively tuned in to your loved one. And yet they still surprise you. Every year brings new challenges but also new pleasures.

Margery Fish writes in *We Made a Garden* (1956) that she developed such intimacy with her plants she saw them as friends. Far from being mere botanical specimens, plants are humanized by gardeners. We have raised, cosseted and nurtured them: no wonder we feel so strongly about them.

In the French classic, *The Little Prince*, the hero has a single rose on the small planet where he lives. He lavishes his love and attention on her, believing her to be unique. When he visits another planet, he comes across a garden filled with roses and is broken-hearted to see that his flower is just the same as the others. But then he realizes something: 'In herself alone she is more important than all the hundreds of you other roses: because it is she that I have watered; because it is she that I have put under the glass globe; because it is she that I have sheltered behind the screen; because it is for her that I have killed the caterpillars (except the two or three that we saved to become butterflies); because it is she that I have listened to, when she grumbled, or boasted, or even sometimes when she said nothing. Because she is my rose.' And then comes this pearl of wisdom: 'It is the time you have wasted for your rose that makes your rose so important.' Gardeners know all about devotion.

*****

After 20 years in my garden, I'm getting to know my plants. A few of the shrubs are getting on a bit. With them I feel an even greater affinity. My old Jacques Cartier rose has seen better days – it's woody and lopsided – but I appreciate it even more than I did in its youth. Every summer it produces scores of perfect flowers. Like a good friend, it is constant. My rugosa is the same. She's a tough old lady, blooming all summer long and redoubling her bounty with plump bright-red hips in the autumn. There are other stalwarts, too: cotoneasters, pyracanthas and a flowering redcurrant, which I planted years ago and have become surprisingly attached to, as if my own gardening roots have slowly and inevitably entwined with theirs.

Even areas that are wiped clean every year bear signs of prolonged love. My veg-flower patch enjoys its rich soil thanks to my annual composting. It might be strange to admit, but there's a bit of me dug in there. It's where I've invested so much of my gardening time and energy, where my hands (and face) have got the most dirty, where my back and knees have bent the longest, where I have nurtured seedlings and weeded with the accuracy of an accountant. So much has come out of this little plot: sweet peas, pumpkins and courgettes, peas, potatoes and sugar snaps, nigellas, cornflowers, dahlias, strawflowers, cosmos and more. Just thinking about it brings me joy. I smile at the thought that its soil holds seeds of beauties that come back every year: blowsy opium poppies, little mounds of forget-me-nots, radiant nasturtiums. If you were to ask me where my gardening heart belonged, I would say in this lovely scrap of soil barely 10ft square.

The garden bears the legacies of previous owners too. Some of these plants I didn't appreciate at first, annoyed at how underwhelming they were. How wrong I was. How could anyone not like the cheering winter blooms of *Viburnum × bodnantense*? Ditto winter jasmine. Ditto early flowering *Crocus tommasinianus*, which lights up my front garden on the first sunny day in February. Now I rejoice at their presence, forever in debt to my gardening predecessor.

When my neighbour died a couple of years ago, I 'inherited' his boundary hedge. It was his pride and joy: a thicket of hawthorn, hazel, holly, privet and beech, beloved of birds. He never let me near it; it was far too precious for anyone else to look after. My new neighbours aren't that attentive to it, so I have adopted the hedge. I trim and weed it with a sort of motherly protection I didn't realize I had in me. Just like the Little Prince with his rose.

'Green fingers are the extension of a verdant heart', writes Russell Page in *The Education of a Gardener* (1962). 'A good garden cannot be made by somebody who has not developed the capacity to know and to love growing things.' Love it certainly is – not the romantic version, but the one that is kind and giving, steady and patient.

I only have to walk around my village and admire the narrow strips of front garden to witness displays of garden love. The little plots aren't just pleasingly pretty; they warm the heart. Someone has spent time tending them, carefully scratching the soil, picking out the weeds and adding a generous layer of mulch. As I walk past them in late March, they are the most gladdening sight I could wish for.

*****

As soon as you start gardening you become part of a large community, even if you have a private plot. Before long, your love of plants will create opportunities for conversation and connection. It could be over the garden fence, in the front garden, on the allotment, during a visit to a garden or nursery, or even online.

The Czech writer and critic Karel Čapek reckoned gardeners could spot each other a mile away. 'I will not betray to you how gardeners recognize one another, whether by smell, or some password, or secret sign; but it is a fact that they recognize one another at first sight,' he writes in *The Gardener's Year* (1931). It's a lovely thought but I'm not sure it's that easy. We're a mixed bunch, there are lots of us, and our numbers are growing. I prefer to think that anyone you meet *could* be a gardener, even if they don't know it yet.

What I do know is that most gardeners are friendly and predictably down to earth. They'll gladly share their knowledge, and many will give away seeds, plants or produce. Maybe it's something to do with the generosity of the plant world. It rubs off on you.

It's amazing what even the tiniest garden gift will do. Last year the stars of my summer garden were tobacco plants from my neighbour. From a handful of inch-tall seedlings, I got masses of flowers and the spectacle, which lasted almost until winter, was made all the more special for having been freely given. My nicotiana weren't just beautiful and heavenly scented blooms; they were uplifting expressions of human kindness.

Every spring someone in my next-door village leaves surplus plants by their house for passers-by to take. Last year I picked up a *Geranium phaeum* – a plant I'd wanted for a while but had never got round to buying. Aside from the delight of getting something for free, there's a unique kind of joy in acquiring a plant that's been handed down. I'm adopting it for my garden, extending the chain of love. Imagine if we were all this generous with our plants. It could be the start of something wonderful.

Actually, something similar is already happening. Every year on the first Sunday in February, gardeners in Brighton gather in the town's Open Market to swap seeds. Launched in 2002, Seedy Sunday is the largest and longest-running seed-swapping event in the UK, but there are lots more

across the country. Seedy Sunday is a social enterprise created for the benefit of the local community and run by volunteers. To take part, you just grab some free Seedy Sunday envelopes and fill them with seeds from your plot. Even if you don't have any seeds to offer, you can buy some on the day, at just 50p a packet.

Seed swaps bring gardeners – experienced and amateur, young and old – together, fostering connections and community, fun and friendship. Volunteers are on hand to offer advice, and there are talks and demonstrations too. As the Seedy Sunday website says: 'For many it marks the start of the gardening year – we come out of hibernation and reconnect with old friends and make new ones.' I can't think of a better way to celebrate the beginning of the growing season than by swapping seeds and spending a little time with other gardeners.

*****

Gardening should be available to everyone, even those without access to land. Guerrilla gardeners have been defending this idea for decades. There are no boundaries for them: vacant plots are there for the taking, each one a chance to fill with flowers, fruit and veg. They spread the gardening love wherever they see horticultural potential, and they see it everywhere: roadsides, tree pits, abandoned or unloved planters, gaps and cracks in pavements, walls.

'We spill out, seeing opportunity to splash colour and character all over the place, tagging the landscape, exhibiting in the street – we are graffiti gardeners,' writes Richard Reynolds in his brilliant book *On Guerrilla Gardening* (2008). More and more people live in cities, with no garden of their own or available plots in which to grow. Guerrilla gardeners fight this scarcity and our rampant urbanization by creating organic environments, however small, wherever they can. In doing so they bring surprise, joy, food and colour to the concrete jungle.

The person credited for starting this movement was New York resident Liz Christy. In 1973, she and a handful of gardening activists founded Green Guerillas. Using seeds as their weapons, they started a gardening revolution, greening up run-down parts of Manhattan. They planted sunflowers wherever they could, adorned tree pits and embellished abandoned buildings with window boxes. They threw 'seed green-aids' (aka seed grenades) over fences and into vacant and derelict lots. They even produced a leaflet showing how to make the bombs, which receptacles to use (Christmas baubles and small balloons were recommended), what to put in them (water, seeds, fertilizer and compost), and techniques on how best to throw the bombs depending on which container you are using. ('For Christmas ornaments – use an underhand throw. For the water balloons – use an overhand throw.')

An abandoned corner plot in Manhattan's Lower East Side came to the group's attention. They climbed over the fence, cleared the site, brought in topsoil and started planting. In 1974, thanks to Liz Christy's campaigning, the City of New York officially approved access to the site for a rent of $1 a month. Soon the newly named Bowery Houston Community Farm and Garden was home to vegetable beds, flower borders and maturing trees. The New York *Daily News* reported: 'They have not only brightened up the corner with flowers and greenery, but have also provided many low-income families in the area with their own fresh produce all summer.'

Green Guerillas became a dynamic social movement, helping instigate other community gardens, running workshops, planting experimental plots to see what could be grown in the city, and hosting plant giveaways. Today the group continues to advocate for access to open green spaces where people can grow their own food, connect with nature, meet and relax. The Bowery Houston Community Farm and Garden is also still running, too, renamed the Liz Christy Garden in honour of its founder.

Community gardens are becoming more and more common in the UK and across the world. Usually, it is thanks to devoted volunteers that they get off the ground and thrive. Their countless acts of kindness build up to create better communities, helping not just to bring food to tables and beauty to previously unloved spots, but making people feel more connected – to each other and nature.

One of the brilliant things about community gardens is that anyone can take part. At Golden Hill Community Garden in Bristol, for example, you turn up and choose what you'd like to do from the day's tasks. It doesn't matter if you've never gardened before or if you have a disability. As its website says, the garden provides 'an inclusive and accessible space and supportive atmosphere where everyone feels valued'. Anyone and everyone is welcome, 'especially volunteers with physical and/or mental ill health or impairments, people with learning difficulties, as well as children and young people'.

Golden Hill came together thanks to a group of local allotment holders who wanted to create a community garden for people who weren't able to get or manage their own plots. The garden has two polytunnels, lots of raised beds and an edible forest with unusual plants, such as Himalayan sea buckthorn and strawberry guava.

'The shared purpose makes it joyful,' says Lucy Mitchell, Golden Hill's community project worker. 'Every time someone does something, it affects all of us – it all adds up to something big. It's amazing how much love and effort has been put into one patch of ground.' Volunteers are encouraged to take away produce at the end of the day; some cook together on site.

There are thousands of community gardens just like Golden Hill, each one contributing to its local area in a special way. It's not just about growing produce, it's about how it makes people feel. 'It's a lovely, natural way to feel part of something, even if you don't interact much,' explains Lucy. 'People come here and leave happier, including me.'

*****

For anyone who shares a love of gardening with a partner, their plot can become a brilliant collaboration. What could be more wonderful than making a garden together? Mirabel Osler certainly saw the appeal. She wanted 'the tentative decisions', 'the shared consultations, the anguishing over expense, the scrappy sketches or fanciful doodlings', and 'that pushing of ideas across the table to each other on winter evenings'. I rather agree with her. I'd also take the sometimes inevitable disagreements over what should go where and who should do what.

For Vita Sackville-West and Harold Nicolson – arguably gardening's most famous couple – Sissinghurst came to reflect their love for each other as well as their different personalities. According to Vita, Harold was the 'ideal collaborator'. He had 'a natural taste for symmetry' and 'an ingenuity in forcing focal points', which she lacked. Vita preferred to concentrate on plants – their shapes, colours and scents; their romantic associations and joyful informality. The couple's complementary talents combined to create a garden of perfect bones and exquisite planting. It was a work of art created by two very different artists.

Little details show just how much the garden was part of Vita and Harold's relationship. During the week, Harold worked in London. As soon as he got back to Sissinghurst on a Friday evening, he would walk around the garden with Vita. She pointed out any changes, having previously left a bunch of flowers for him to find in his room. And on Monday mornings, Harold went back to London laden with flowers from the garden. In 1936 he writes to Vita from the city: 'Irises do not care for the Southern Railway. On the other hand, lupins travel lovely and the syringa does not turn a hair .... I have bought some bigger and better vases to house my flowers. They are such a pleasure to me.' Theirs was an open marriage – both had many same-sex relationships during their life together – but in their garden Vita and Harold found a point of communion. Sissinghurst was their longest, and joint, love affair.

In 1938, eight years after having bought Sissinghurst, Vita first opened the garden to the public. She did so through the National Garden Scheme (NGS), which had been created in 1927 with the aim of 'opening gardens of quality, character and interest to the public for charity'. The entrance fee being a shilling, Vita called visitors her 'shillingses'. She enjoyed talking and sharing her love for Sissinghurst with them. Writing in the *New Statesman* in 1939, she says: 'Between them and myself a particular form of courtesy survives, a gardener's courtesy, in a world where courtesy is giving place to rougher things.' I believe this civility is a common experience for anyone who visits an NGS garden today. It's definitely something I've felt: that respect and kindred feeling for a fellow gardener who has put so much love into their plot and is happy to share it for a few hours in support of a good cause: yet another example of how gardening brings people together.

Aside from being a stimulating creative pursuit, gardening with a partner also offers one of the best forms of companionship: the silent one. You're working together but separately – just like in a community garden – towards a shared goal. You might be weeding a border and your partner mowing the lawn, but you feel connected in your work.

Virginia Woolf wasn't a gardener – her husband Leonard was – but she enjoyed doing the straightforward tasks such as digging, weeding and picking fruit and veg. Gardening, like walking, was the ideal counterpoint to the couple's writing life. 'In the morning we write 750 words, in the afternoon we dig,' Leonard writes to his friend Lytton Strachey.

As you'd expect, the couple also enjoyed moments of shared contemplation in the garden. One of their favourite pastimes was simply looking at the fish. 'It is our passion to observe the gold fish,' Virginia writes in 1931. 'There should be four, and one carp; but it is the rarest event to see them all together – and yet I can assure you that to see them matters more to us both than all that is said at the Hague.' The garden was their escape – a snug, verdant cocoon that held them buffeted from the stresses of the world. Maybe sometimes it felt like they were surrounded – to use Virginia's famous phrase – by a luminous halo.

Virginia once asked: 'What do you think is probably the happiest moment in one's whole life?' She answered the question herself: 'I think it's the moment when one is walking in one's garden, perhaps picking off a few dead flowers, and then suddenly one thinks: My husband lives in that house – and he loves me.' Imagining herself in her garden, Virginia brings to mind her love for Leonard.

It's a natural connection to make. Gardens are inhabited by loved ones, present and past. Like our homes, our gardens are profoundly resonant, filled with treasured moments and memories, accumulated thoughts and feelings. Often these are brought back by the tiniest thing. Like, for instance, when I found an old Matchbox car hiding behind a shrub in my garden. It had been lying there, rusting away, for years. A vision of my toddler son came flooding back, so precise I could almost feel him breathing next to me. There he was, with his straw-blond curls, blue eyes and dirty chubby fingers, pushing his car back and forth along the top of the patio wall. He'd spend hours doing this, entranced by the motion of the wheels, in a world of his own.

Smell, we all know, is a great releaser of memories and there are so many scents in our gardens, especially those of our childhood. I only have to sniff a bay leaf and I'm back in my grandparents' garden in Sussex. As a young girl, a favourite spot for playing hide and seek was between a large bay hedge and the shed. While I waited for my sister to find me, I'd pick a leaf and fold it in half to release the aroma. Just thinking about it brings back a rush of memories. By the shed was the veg patch where my grandmother grew runner beans and the most beautiful flowers I'd ever set eyes on: delicate pink and salmon clarkias, which I now grow in my own garden and will remind me of her, always. Against a nearby wall there was a fig tree that had me spellbound. Partly it was those bold, exotic-looking, oversized leaves, but mostly it was the figs. They promised so much, but sadly never delivered. Every summer I hoped one would be ripe enough to eat. I was never there at the right time.

In my mind's eye I am now walking down the lawn towards my grandfather's little rose bed, filled with proud hybrid teas. It was here – in the sunniest part of the garden – that we would gather for our daily ritual of tea and cake. For a young girl from the Paris suburbs, tea in an English garden was a treat and a novelty (so too were fish fingers and baked beans). While my grandmother cheerfully poured tea into chintz cups, behind her a pretty *Rosa* 'Albertine' clothed the red-brick walls of the house, its pink blooms like frilly tutus to my ballet-loving young self. It felt like a scene in a picture book.

They were halcyon holidays. We went on blackberry-picking expeditions, trips to the seaside, long forest walks. But the most magical moments were often closer to home: making mud pies, tunnelling my way behind shrubberies, searching for pine cones and other natural treasures, taking sneaky shortcuts through the hedge to visit my friend next door. Flowers stand out too: mounds of soft-toned heathers, especially the adorable bell heathers (*Erica cinerea*); waves of swaying crocosmia whose blooms made me think of exotic birds; and so many sweetly scented and butterfly-bejewelled buddleias.

After two weeks of English food and fun, it was time to go home. The scent of departure was always that of Mexican orange, courtesy of a big shrub next to my grandparents' front door. Since then, its fragrant leaves have had a bitter-sweet association.

Memories, like my lovely old shrubs, have long roots in gardens. Before you know it, you can find yourself retrieving lost loved ones – friends, grandparents and children who are now all grown up, including yourself.

Happiness

'Weeding all day to finish the beds, in a queer sort of enthusiasm which made me say this is happiness'.

VIRGINIA WOOLF

———————————

Virginia Woolf wrote these words in 1920, less than a year after she bought Monk's House. Has she suddenly realized that gardening is enjoyable, a source of happiness, even? I'd like to think so. When it dawns on you that working in a garden brings joy, a deep well of contentment presents itself to you. Sometimes it can take years to fully appreciate how much fun can be had from getting your hands dirty, that even the grind of a few hours of weeding can be deeply satisfying.

For me this dawning appreciation was coupled with a radiant feeling, which is often repeated when I spend time in the garden. It doesn't always happen – sometimes I'm too distracted or time-poor – but when it does it feels like a blessing. A mood takes over and I'm slowly permeated with a wonderful sense of wellbeing. At best it can be like a waking dream, where everything is bathed in beauty and goodness. Then even the weeds and all the unsightly bits of the garden and small annoyances such as neighbourly noises will not dent my mood. I am imperturbably happy.

Why? Who knows? So much is at play. But what I do know is that this state of being is hard to beat, and it isn't superficial. After all, it is based on firm ground, relies on a connection to place and body-and-mind engagement. Unlike listening to music or watching TV, gardening asks something of you, but the payback for participation is more profound and longer lasting.

Charles Dudley Warner understood this feeling well. 'How many hours, how many minutes, does one get of that pure content which is happiness?' he wonders in *My Summer in a Garden* (1870). 'I do not mean laziness, which is always discontent; but the serene enjoyment, in which all the natural senses have easy play, and the unnatural ones have a holiday. There is probably nothing that has such a tranquillizing effect, and leads into such content, as gardening.'

Gertrude Jekyll was also keen to share gardening's positive effects: 'The lesson I have thoroughly learnt, and wish to pass on to others, is to know the enduring happiness that the love of a garden gives.' The problem is it isn't something that can be taught. You have to experience it for yourself.

*****

Like Virginia Woolf, I'm prone to melancholy. In the midst of a low mood, I sometimes forget where to find happiness; things lose their appeal. At times like these the garden can feel like a burden. But if I stop and think – rather than let myself be overtaken by my own despondency – I know that gardening is a lifeboat for low mood. If I put a little effort in, if I jolt myself into action, I can get myself unstuck. Slowly, I get wrapped up in the process and start to appreciate the here and now. Maybe this is how Virginia felt when she was overtaken by her 'queer sort of enthusiasm'. She's right: it is rather strange to enjoy weeding and other such tasks. But gardeners know that these jobs can break the vicious cycle of low spirits. After a few minutes of weeding, I can be riding a tiny yet growing wave of optimism.

Every year, there's a day – usually in April – when I'm drawn into the garden for no particular reason. I might start hand-weeding a patch of seedlings in the border. The weather is mild and the soil warmer than it's felt for ages. All around me are signs of emerging life: the ferns are unfurling; fresh clematis stems are reaching skywards in search of supports; the tulips are in full pomp and the lilac about to burst. My two cats are chasing each other across the lawn, shamelessly displaying their delight at having me on their turf. The sun has come out and is heating my back, easing some of the winter tension. That's when – in splendid fullness – I remember why I love gardening. I can see the whole summer stretch before me. Soon my seeds will be emerging, promising old favourites such as cosmos and scabious, alongside new attempts (this year, hopefully, I will enjoy a haze of *Ammi majus* and candy-coloured zinnias). My recently potted dahlia tubers will be sprouting in a few days. In my mind's eye I can already see them casting their pompom shapes and pastel shades against the azure sky.

I continue my reverie. Before long, my bamboo wigwams will be decked in sweet peas and the summer sun will be working its magic, saturating the plume poppies and hops with a magical glow. And the bats will be back for their evening acrobatics, joining me on my nightly waterings. I look forward to those clear summer mornings when I go into the garden barefoot to enjoy the stillness of the air and the promise of the day.

Celia Thaxter recounts a similar experience: 'When in these fresh mornings I go into my garden before any one is awake, I go for the time being into perfect happiness. ... The fair face of every flower salutes me with a silent joy that fills me with infinite content; each gives me its color, its grace, its perfume, and enriches me with the consummation of its beauty. All the cares, perplexities, and griefs of existence, all the burdens of life slip

from my shoulders and leave me with the heart of a little child that asks nothing beyond its present moment of innocent bliss.'

Some days in the garden are so heavenly that I can catch myself wondering why I ever booked a summer holiday. I feel vexed and guilty that I will be deserting it for a week. Why would I leave all this when escape is right here? Filled with praise and thankfulness for her plot, Celia Thaxter enthuses: 'This little island garden of mine is so small that the amount of pure delight it gives in the course of a summer is something hardly to be credited.' Even the smallest garden – it might not even be a garden – can afford a host of pleasures and bring about contentment and quietness of mind, meaning that happiness, for the gardener, is always close at hand.

Of course, it isn't just about those blissful summer days where everything comes together. Gardeners hold the essence of their garden within their hearts so that, even in the darkness of winter or during difficult times, it is a source of comfort and nourishment. Its presence suggests itself, sometimes at the most unexpected of moments. At times it's felt as if my garden was actually holding me safe in its hull, steering me through choppy waters.

*****

Happiness can mean so many different things, but I think most of us would acknowledge that it isn't just about experiencing pleasant sensations or feelings. Many philosophers have argued that, rather than reflecting a momentary state of subjective wellbeing, happiness relates to something deeper. 'One swallow does not make a summer, neither does one day,' Aristotle famously writes in his *Nicomachean Ethics* (350 bc). 'Similarly neither can one day, or a brief space of time, make a man blessed and happy.' It's the whole picture that counts. So that, when you ask yourself 'Am I happy?', your answer will be a considered and holistic assessment of your life, not an indication of your current mood. The question might prompt you to think about what actually makes you happy and lead to questions about your values and purpose in life.

For Aristotle, happiness is linked to *eudaimonia*, which broadly means 'human flourishing'. For him, the happy life is the one in which you exercise your capacities through worthwhile activities done well. Rather than being a state you reach, happiness is something you do. You cultivate it, just like you cultivate a garden. It's an activity, just like gardening.

In *Philosophies of Happiness: A Comparative Approach to the Flourishing Life* (2017), Diana Lobel, Associate Professor of Religion at Boston University, considers the idea of happiness or human flourishing from a cross-cultural perspective. She looks at traditions ranging from Aristotle, Augustine and Maimonides to Confucianism, Daoism, the *Bhagavad Gītā* and Japanese Zen Buddhism. As she writes in her introduction: 'These traditions and approaches to a flourishing life are quite diverse, but certain themes will emerge.' Through her research, she identifies six building blocks for happiness:

1. Attentive awareness. 'Happiness includes appreciation of the beauty and value of our moment-to-moment experience. Rather than rushing to the next, more valuable activity, we can pause and appreciate the spaciousness and value of the present-moment awareness.'
2. Effortless ease of action, so that one is guided by intuitive wisdom in what we do – a bit like the concept of flow. 'This brings vitality and efficacy to our activities.'
3. Relationship and connection. 'Humans need to feel part of a larger, interconnected whole.'
4. Love or devotion. 'Human beings connect to the whole not only with the mind but affectively, with the heart and spirit.'
5. Creative engagement. 'Human beings flourish when we draw upon the full range of our resources and fully participate in the projects of our lives.'
6. Meaning, significance and value. 'Flourishing lives have objective import, worth, and purpose.'

If leading a happy life involves all of the above, then gardeners are doing okay. As I hope the chapters in this book have shown, gardening encompasses all of these building blocks. By engaging our five senses, it offers countless opportunities to tune into the natural world, to our sensations, and to the fundamental yet amazing fact of being alive. Its many simple tasks help us to slow down, bringing about present-moment awareness, greater mental space and inner peace. And while we engage in these activities, we experience that wonderful sense of flow – or as Lobel calls it, ease of action – which makes us feel fully alive and capable.

Gardening brings us into contact with the outside world – plants, animals, the elements, the seasons – making us feel part of the rich web of life. It can foster connection and friendship with fellow gardeners, too. And because we are devoted to our plots, gardening always involves matters of the heart while keeping us creatively engaged and curious. Finally, gardeners have a purpose in life. Like the Little Prince, we have something special to look after. We can even find what Lobel calls 'objective import' by gardening for nature and wildlife; by giving away seeds, plants and produce; by volunteering for a local community garden or a gardening charity.

Because happiness is a skill, you can become so good at it that it permeates every part of your life. In *Happiness: A Guide to Developing Life's Most Important Skill* (2006), French Buddhist monk Matthieu Ricard says that happiness 'is not a mere pleasurable feeling, a fleeting emotion, or a mood, but an optimal state of being' which 'defines the quality of every moment of our lives'. I believe gardeners are well placed to reach this state of being; it's no surprise that many of the horticultural professions – from gardening to floristry to landscape design – rank highly in happiness and job-satisfaction surveys. It is proof, too, that money and high status are not the answers to a happy life, even though these are the things many people identify as being the solution to their unhappiness.

I'll leave you with these words by my favourite garden-poet Derek Jarman, from his diary *Modern Nature* (2018): 'And finally I found my passion: the garden ... the crucial thing, for survival of the spirit, is to look for that passion, and cleave to it with all your might. Then, somehow, everything will be all right.' Once gardening has taken hold of you, it won't let you go.

BIBLIOGRAPHY

Bardsley, Barney, *A Handful of Earth: A Year of Healing and Growing*, John Murray, 2008

Čapek, Karel, *The Gardener's Year*, George Allen & Unwin, 1931

Cook, E. T., *Gardens of England*, A. & C. Black, 1908

Cooper, David E., *A Philosophy of Gardens*, Oxford University Press, 2006

Don, Monty, *My Roots*, Two Roads, 2006

Don, Monty and Sarah, *The Jewel Garden*, Two Roads, 2005

Farrell, Holly, *Gardening for Mindfulness*, Mitchell Beazley, 2017

Fish, Margery, *We Made a Garden*, Collingridge, 1956

Gross, Harriet, *The Psychology of Gardening*, Routledge, 2018

Hamilton, Jill, Penny Hart, and John Simmons, *The Gardens of William Morris*, Frances Lincoln, 2006

Hobhouse, Penelope, *The Story of Gardening*, Dorling Kindersley, 2002

Holmes, Caroline, *Monet at Giverny*, Weidenfeld & Nicolson, 2003

Jarman, Derek, *Derek Jarman's Garden*, Thames and Hudson, 1995

Jarman, Derek, *Modern Nature*, Vintage Classics, 2018

Jekyll, Gertrude, *Colour in the Flower Garden*, Country Life, 1908

Jekyll, Gertrude, *Wood and Garden: Notes and Thoughts, Practical and Critical, of a Working Amateur*, Longmans, 1899

Le Lièvre, Audrey, *Miss Willmott of Warley Place: Her Life and Her Gardens*, Faber and Faber, 2008

Lobel, Diana, *Philosophies of Happiness: A Comparative Approach to the Flourishing Life*, Columbia University Press, 2017

Loudon, Jane, *Instructions in Gardening for Ladies*, John Murray, 1840

Naydler, Jeremy, *Gardening as a Sacred Art: Towards a Redemption of our Relationship with Nature*, Floris Books, 2011

O'Brien, Dan (ed.), *Gardening: Philosophy for Everyone*, Wiley-Blackwell, 2010

Orwell, George, *Diaries*, Penguin Classics, 2010

Osler, Mirabel, *A Breath from Elsewhere: Musings on Gardens*, Bloomsbury, 1998

Osler, Mirabel, *A Gentle Plea for Chaos: Reflections from an English Garden*, Bloomsbury, 1989

Osler, Mirabel, *In the Eye of the Garden*, J. M. Dent, 1993

Oudolf, Piet and Noel Kingsbury, *Planting: A New Perspective*, Timber Press, 2013

Owen, Jennifer, *Wildlife of a Garden: A Thirty-Year Study*, Royal Horticultural Society, 2010

Page, Russell, *The Education of a Gardener*, William Collins, 1962

Pearson, Dan, *Natural Selection*, Guardian Faber Publishing, 2017

Pollan, Michael, *Second Nature: A Gardener's Education*, Black Cat, 2003

Purdom, C. B. *The Garden City: A Study in the Development of the Modern Town*, J. M. Dent & Sons, 1913

Reynolds, Richard, *On Guerrilla Gardening: A Handbook for Gardening without Boundaries*, Bloomsbury Publishing, 2008

Ricard, Matthieu, *Happiness: A Guide to Developing Life's Most Important Skill*, Little, Brown & Company, 2006

Russell, Vivian, *Monet's Garden: Through the Seasons at Giverny*, Frances Lincoln, 2016

Sedding, John D., *Garden-Craft Old and New*, Kegan Paul, 1891

Stuart-Smith, Sue, *The Well-Gardened Mind*, William Collins, 2020

Tankard, Judith, and Martin Wood, *Gertrude Jekyll at Munstead Wood*, Bramley Books, 1998

Thaxter, Celia, *An Island Garden*, 1894

Vogt, Benjamin, *A New Garden Ethic: Cultivating Defiant Compassion for an Uncertain Future*, New Society Publishers, 2017

Voltaire, *Candide, or Optimism* (translated by Theo Cuff), Penguin Classics, 2006

Von Arnim, Elizabeth, *Elizabeth and Her German Garden*, Penguin Classics, 2008

Warner, Charles Dudley, *My Summer in a Garden*, James R. Osgood & Co., 1870

Wheeler, David (ed.), *The Penguin Book of Garden Writing*, Penguin Books, 1996

Young, Damon, *Philosophy in the Garden*, Scribe, 2020

Zoob, Caroline, *Virginia Woolf's Garden: The Story of the Garden at Monk's House*, Jacqui Small, 2013

INDEX

ACKNOWLEDGEMENTS

Thank you to Editorial Director Peter Taylor for believing in my proposal. As a fellow gardener, I hope you'll enjoy reading the finished article. Thanks also to Batsford's brilliant publishing team, especially Tina Persaud and Kristy Richardson: you turned my manuscript into a beautiful book. Claire Harrup, your illustrations are just perfect; I am grateful and delighted to have them next to my words.

Many thanks to Barney Bardsley for allowing me to quote from your beautiful memoir, *A Handful of Earth*, and for all your kind messages; to Vicky – for your constant friendship and all the adventures; to Franco – for regularly checking in, for your support and dark humour. And with gratitude, as ever, to Mum, for always being there, and to Alex, for keeping it real.

In memory of Jill and Izzy, who died during the writing of this book.